ECOLOGY AND EVOLUTION
ISLANDS OF CHANGE

NATIONAL SCIENCE TEACHERS ASSOCIATION

Shirley Watt Ireton, Director
Beth Daniels, Managing Editor
Erin Miller, Associate Editor
Jessica Green, Assistant Editor
Anne Early, Editorial Assistant
Cara Young, Copyeditor
Linda Olliver, Cover Design

Art and Design
Kim Alberto, Director
NSTA Web
Tim Weber, Webmaster
Outreach
Michael Byrnes, Editor-at-Large
Periodicals Publishing
Shelley Carey, Director
Printing and Production
Catherine Lorrain-Hale, Director
Publications Operations
Erin Miller, Manager
sciLINKS
Tyson Brown, Manager

National Science Teachers Association
Gerald F. Wheeler, Executive Director
David Beacom, Publisher

NSTA Press, NSTA Journals, and the NSTA
Web site deliver high-quality resources for
science educators.

Ecology and Evolution: Islands of Change
NSTA stock number: PB153X
ISBN 0-87355-183-4
Library of Congress Control Number: 00-132231
Printed in the USA by Automated Graphics Systems, Inc.
Printed on recycled paper.

Photographs by William F. McComas

Many of the ideas in this volume appeared in an earlier version in *The Galápagos: JASON Curriculum*, ©1991 by the
National Science Teachers Association. This publication also provided some of the source material for a teacher's guide,
poster, and Web site developed by NSTA on behalf of the Smithsonian Institution for the IMAX film *Galapagos in 3D*.
Permission has been granted by the Smithsonian to further develop those materials in this volume.

ECOLOGY AND EVOLUTION
ISLANDS OF CHANGE

Written and Adapted by
Richard Benz

Featuring *sci*LINKS®—a new way of connecting text and the Internet. Up-to-the-minute online content, classroom ideas, and other materials are just a click away. Go to page xii to learn more about this new educational resource.

NATIONAL SCIENCE TEACHERS ASSOCIATION
ARLINGTON, VIRGINIA

TABLE OF CONTENTS

GALÁPAGOS: FRAME OF REFERENCE

ECOLOGY AND ISLANDS

EVOLUTION

ABOUT THE AUTHOR

Richard Benz has taught science for 27 years at Wickliffe High School in Lake County, Ohio. During those years he has taught four levels of biology, Earth science, photography, and a science research course, and has served as the science chair since 1978. In addition to teaching at Wickliffe, he teaches in-service classes to teachers throughout the country in science, science proficiency, technology, and teaching with the Internet. Mr. Benz is currently teaching an Internet course that deals with evolution and the nature of science, as part of the Virtual High School project.

The Ohio Academy of Science recently inducted Mr. Benz as a Fellow, and in 1987 named him Ohio Science Teacher of the Year. Mr. Benz also received the Presidential Award for Excellence in Science and Mathematics Teaching in 1990, in 1996 was selected Outstanding Biology Teacher of America for Ohio by the National Association of Biology Teachers, received the Ohio Milken National Award in 1992, and the Disney American Teacher Award in Science in 1993. He has also won recognition for his work mixing media in the classroom, including the Internet and educational television.

ACKNOWLEDGMENTS

Richard Benz would like to dedicate this book to three key influences:

- First, to my wife Betsy—my biggest promoter and greatest cheerleader.
- Next, to Walter Hintz, my high school biology teacher, friend, fellow explorer, the best field naturalist I have ever met, and the man who introduced me to the ideas of Darwin, Mendel, and Watson and Crick.
- Finally, to Charles Darwin himself, a great observer, an incredible thinker, and an originator of ideas that "shook the world of science."

NSTA would like to thank the many people who contributed to the development of this book: Marily DeWall, Frank Watt Ireton and the team who developed *The Galápagos: JASON Curriculum* which provided a basis for this project; Laura McKie and Carole Baldwin of the Smithsonian Institution for their work on this material and the associated *Galapagos in 3D* projects; reviewers Sue Cassidy, E. Barbara Klemm, Sharon Radford, Irwin L. Slesnick; field testers Johanna Brandriff, Suzanne Cook, Mary Haskins, Vince Iacovelli, Steve Rich, Marilyn Rightor, Carol L. St. Clair, and Cecilia Wilson; and artist Max-Karl Winkler. Special thanks goes to Tui de Roy for her input. *Ecology and Evolution: Islands of Change* is produced by NSTA Press: Shirley Watt Ireton, director; Beth Daniels, managing editor; Erin Miller, associate editor; Jessica Green, assistant editor; Anne Early, editorial assistant. Erin Miller is the project editor for *Ecology and Evolution: Islands of Change*. Copyediting by Cara Young; cover design by Linda Olliver.

INTRODUCTION

Thus each separate island of the Galápagos Archipelago is tenanted, and the fact is a marvelous one, by many distinct species; but these species are related to each other in a very much closer manner than to the inhabitants of the American continent, or of any other quarter of the world. This is what might have been expected, for islands situated so near to each other would almost necessarily receive immigrants from the same original source, and from each other. But how is it that many of the immigrants have been differently modified, though only in a small degree, in islands situated within sight of each other, having the same geological nature, the same height, climate, etc.?

Charles Darwin, *On the Origin of Species by Means of Natural Selection*, 1872

Recently, science teaching has been criticized by both professional educators and scientists because all too often science is taught as a huge collection of disconnected definitions and facts that must be rote memorized. Of course this is not science; science is just the opposite—a collection of interwoven themes and explanations that help us to understand the natural world. The process of science is not a process of memorizing facts, it is a process of gathering information, observing, testing explanations, and developing understandings. Evolution is one of these very important interwoven and investigated themes. An understanding of evolutionary concepts is crucial for explaining the natural world of the past and the present. Students should not only be introduced to evolution in their science classes, but also must understand how the concept pervades and helps explain much of science. Without this applied connection, evolution is just another definition on paper.

This book is an exploration of ecology and evolution, two of the most important processes in biology. The activities help students investigate these interwoven biological themes by using the Galápagos Islands as a case study. Although ecology by itself is a "hot" topic of study, and is certainly far less contentious than evolution, often the two are taught as unconnected units. The goal of *Ecology and Evolution: Islands of Change* is to demonstrate how the two subjects are inherently linked: how environmental forces influence interactions between organisms and potentially lead to changes that shape the diversity of life on Earth. Although most of the activities can be taught independently, we hope they are taught as a cohesive unit to better illustrate how these elements are intertwined.

The Nature of Science

Part of the problem with the perception of science as a complex collection of unrelated definitions is vocabulary that has multiple meanings. Terms such as *hypothesis*, *theory*, and *law* are common culprits, because these words can have different meanings in everyday speech. Although many people use hypothesis to mean a random guess, scientifically, a hypothesis is a statement that can be tested through various experiments and observations, and then accepted or rejected.

Hypotheses that have not been rejected are used to create theories that explain some aspect of the natural world. A theory is an explanation that is well tested and substantiated by experiments and observations. Although commonly used to mean a belief (such as "I have a theory it will snow today"), in science, a theory is not something that is "believed," it is an explanation based on evidence. A scientific law is a statement that describes how some part of the natural world works or behaves, based on theories and hypotheses that have not been rejected through experiments. Science is a way of understanding the world based on confirmable data (data obtained through observations and experiments and verified by others); phenomena that can be observed, measured, and explained by empirical evidence.

That evolution is a theory means it is based on a great deal of evidence; a fact that is often lost in debate. Evolution is the explanation for what causes the incredible diversity of life on this planet; it is a means of connecting all living organisms. Evolution is, in fact, the central theme of biology.

Science is not a system of thinking that involves believing or not believing in something—it is a system of thinking based on observations, experiments, and evidence. Some teachers explain this concept by telling their students that they can "believe" in whatever they wish because believing in something requires faith. They cannot "believe" in evolution, they can only accept it or reject it based on evidence, as they would with any other scientific theory, such as the theory of gravity or the theory that the planets move around the sun in elliptical orbits. The scientific community accepts the theory of evolution as the explanation of how organisms change over time. A good source of reading on this subject is *The Creation Controversy & The Science Classroom*, published by NSTA.

Why the Galápagos Islands?

As Charles Darwin duly noted in the name of his landmark publication, *On the Origin of Species by Means of Natural Selection*, the environment is at the heart of the evolutionary process. Darwin's visit to the Galápagos Islands spawned the ideas in *Origin of Species*. In my own travels to the Galápagos over the past decade, I have been treated to firsthand observations of the influences that the environment has on organisms.

During my first visit in 1994 I was treated to a colony of blue-footed boobies taking advantage of the rich marine flora and fauna that prevailed that year. Almost every nest on Española Island had two "booby babies" in it. Blue-footed boobies are known for a behavior called *facultative siblicide*. Facultative siblicide is when a bird lays two eggs a number of days apart. The first bird to hatch has an advantage for survival because it starts feeding—and therefore growing—sooner. Eventually, the bigger bird pushes the younger, smaller bird from the nest, killing it. The behavior is *facultative* (taking place under certain circumstances) in blue-footed boobies because it occurs when there is not enough food to support both birds. If the food supply is unusually large, both chicks can survive. However, a similar behavior is found in the masked booby, but it is *obligatory siblicide*, that is, the second hatchling is eliminated even in years of abundance, with enough food to support both. In 1994, there was abundant food for the boobies. During subsequent visits I found the masked booby nests on Española had only one living hatchling. When I visited this island after the 1997–98 El Niño event, very few boobies were on their nests at all. Thus, the environment is a very important factor in determining the survivability of the young blue-footed boobies.

Island ecosystems have long been thought of as special places for the study of scientific phenomena. The origins of islands were a topic of study of great naturalists such as Charles Lyell, Robert Wallace, and Charles Darwin almost two centuries ago. More recently, books such as *The Theory of Island Biogeography* by Robert MacArthur and Edward O. Wilson focus on islands as "living laboratories."

The Galápagos Islands made a perfect case study for this book, partly because the archipelago is situated almost 1,000 km from the nearest mainland, partly because the islands are geologically new landforms, and partly because they lie at the intersection of two very important ocean currents: the Humboldt (or Peru) Current and the Panama Current. Furthermore, the Galápagos have been connected to evolutionary studies ever since Darwin. Since publication of *Origin of Species* in 1859, the Galápagos have been used as a natural laboratory for the study of interplay between evolutionary changes and ecological variations.

The Galápagos Islands are used as a running theme throughout the book to help students understand the connections between evolution and ecology. The first chapter of the book "sets the stage" for the rest of the activities. These activities cover the importance of the Galápagos in both time and place, or in other words, the geography and the history of the islands. Next, the ecology of the islands is connected to the forces of change (such as volcanic eruptions, ocean currents, and weather patterns) that have been sculpting the Galápagos since they first emerged from the great Pacific Ocean as volcanic masses waiting to be populated with "new beings." Finally, students will investigate the actual mechanism of change. Natural selection, adaptation, and the genetic influences on evolution are presented in the form of games, allowing students to learn while they play. *Ecology and Evolution: Islands of Change* allows teachers and students to explore the where, the how, the why, and finally, the what of evolution and ecology in the Galápagos Islands.

How to Use this Book

Ecology and Evolution: Islands of Change is neither a textbook nor a lab book; it is intended as a supplement to an existing science class, preferably an integrated science class. It can be used as the main set of activities in a nine-week unit on island biogeography, or on ecology in general. The nature of science lends itself to integration of the many disciplines we have come to recognize as the core curriculum in science: biology, chemistry, Earth science, and physical science. The variety of activities included in *Ecology and Evolution* show that integration. In fact, the whole concept of island science is a perfect starting point for an integrated course. We investigate the Earth science concepts that help explain the formation of the various islands, as well as the physical science principles that govern the currents which daily and annually influence the islands. The climate of the region directly affects the flora and the fauna that is found on the island. The integration of concepts (that we separate into disciplines or areas of study) that governs the natural world can be studied easily with islands as the centerpiece. As an added benefit, the activities are linked to the Internet through *sci*LINKS (see page xii for more information).

Standards and Assessment

The focus of *Ecology and Evolution* is on student discovery and inquiry; as outlined in the goals of the *National Science Education Standards*, students will

- experience the richness and excitement of knowing about and understanding the natural world;
- use appropriate scientific processes and principles in making personal decisions;
- engage intelligently in public discourse and debate about matters of scientific and technological concern; and
- increase their economic productivity through the use of the knowledge, understanding, and skills of the scientifically literate person in their careers.

INTRODUCTION

As stated in the introduction to the *Standards*,

> [S]chools that implement the Standards *will have students learning science by actively engaging in inquiries that are interesting and important to them. Students thereby will establish a knowledge base for understanding science. In these schools, teachers will be empowered to make decisions about what students learn, how they learn it, and how resources are allocated.*

These ideas are the underpinnings of this text. The students will learn about science by practicing many of the skills embodied in the process of science itself.

The *Standards* emphasize the active nature of learning science. The oft-used expression "hands-on science" is only a portion of the activity of science. The *Standards* also note the importance of "minds-on" activities. This book goes beyond simple hands-on activities, making every attempt to involve students in "inquiry-oriented investigations in which they interact with their teachers and peers." The author and editors intend students to use these activities to establish connections between their current knowledge of science and the scientific knowledge found within these pages. We hope students will apply the science content in each activity to new questions as they engage in problem-solving, planning, decision-making, and group discussions.

The embedded assessments are consistent with this active approach to learning. Each activity emphasizes group investigation of the important concepts. This approach is consistent with the recommended teaching strategies from the *Standards*.

• Student understanding is actively constructed through individual and social processes.

In the same way that scientists develop their knowledge and understanding as they seek answers to questions about the natural world, students develop an understanding of the natural world when they are actively engaged in scientific inquiry—both individually and in groups.

As explained in the *Standards*, science itself is a collaborative activity that depends on the ultimate sharing and debating of ideas. The teacher needs to guide student groups to ensure full participation by all members of the group. The interactions within and between groups in the classroom encourage understanding of scientific concepts and the nature of scientific endeavors. Each activity includes teacher-guiding strategies and suggestions on how to incorporate group work. Of course, the individual teacher must decide the teaching strategy for each activity, whether it be through individual work, small group collaboration, or whole class instruction.

Not only is teaching strategy an important component of the educational process, assessment also must be included in any instructional plan. Hence, each activity in *Ecology and Evolution* includes assessment suggestions. For example, in Activity 8, *Arrival Of Life*, students investigate a number of possible explanations for how organisms colonized the remote Galápagos Islands. The rubric for this activity (shown below) demonstrates the general structure of all the rubrics included in the book. Each activity is listed with three levels of assessment: Exemplary, Emergent, and Deficient. Below each level of assessment is a sample description of student accomplishment expected at the particular level.

Activity	Exemplary	Emergent	Deficient
	Students develop a testable hypothesis of how seeds could have colonized the newly formed Galápagos Islands. They are able to design and complete an experiment to test their hypothesis. Finally they are able to connect their results to their original hypothesis.	Students have some trouble coming up with a testable hypothesis. With some help they are able to complete their research.	Students have difficulty developing a hypothesis and carrying out their experiments. They need help and direction throughout the activity, and do not understand how organisms could have colonized the new Galápagos Islands.

Teachers are welcome to use the rubrics included in each activity, but are invited to create their own. The rubrics included are designed to give teachers suggestions on how to include assessments in their teaching strategies.

Finally, should teachers use all of the activities in this book? Of course they should! I think they are all great activities. They comprise a full study of evolution, the history of evolutionary thought, the integration of geology and evolution, the impact of climate on evolution, the importance of ecology on evolution, and ultimately the special circumstances that surround the biogeography of islands. But can teachers use some activities and not others? They can pick the activities that supplement their curriculum. They can use activities that enhance specific concepts, including ecology, geology, meteorology, oceanography, biology, etc. The book is organized such that each activity leads into the next, but can also stand alone. If students need additional information to complete a particular exercise, the teacher can refer to an earlier activity.

The first chapter, *Galápagos: Frame of Reference*, helps to establish the geography of islands in general, and the Galápagos Islands specifically. It also helps students understand the geologic history as well as the human history of these islands. With this background, the second chapter, *Ecology and Islands,* introduces students to the geology that is responsible for the formation of many archipelagos around the world and the oceanographic and the climatic influences on islands. The interrelationship of island ecology and the forces that influence evolution is the main objective of the third chapter, *Evolution.* Here students are introduced to the concepts of biological classification, simple genetics, adaptation of organisms, and natural selection, in order to establish a functional understanding of evolution and evolutionary processes. The most important aspect of *Ecology and Evolution: Islands of Change* is the way that these topics are presented—hands-on, inquiry-oriented laboratories and activities. Not only are these teaching strategies recommended by the *National Science Education Standards,* they are strategies that work. I hope that this book will help your students understand the interconnections of ecological principles and evolutionary concepts *and* discover the excitement of these wonderful *Islands of Change*!

Richard Benz, Wickliffe High School
April 2000

Ecology and Evolution: Islands of Change brings you *sci*LINKS, a new project that blends the two main delivery systems for curriculum—books and telecommunications—into a dynamic new educational tool for children, their parents, and their teachers. *sci*LINKS links specific science content with instructionally-rich Internet resources. *sci*LINKS represents an enormous opportunity to create new pathways for learners, new opportunities for professional growth among teachers, and new modes of engagement for parents.

In this *sci*LINKed text, you will find an icon near several of the concepts you are studying. Under it, you will find the *sci*LINKS URL (http://www.scilinks.org/) and a code. Go to the *sci*LINKS Web site, sign in, type the code from your text, and you will receive a list of URLs that are selected by science educators. Sites are chosen for accurate and age-appropriate content and good pedagogy. The underlying database changes constantly, eliminating dead or revised sites or simply replacing them with better selections. The ink may dry on the page, but the science it describes will always be fresh. *sci*LINKS also ensures that the online content teachers count on remains available for the life of this text. The *sci*LINKS search team regularly reviews the materials to which this text points—revising the URLs as needed or replacing Web pages that have disappeared with new pages. When you send your students to *sci*LINKS to use a code from this text, you can always count on good content being available.

Topic: Galápagos Islands

Go to: www.scilinks.org

Code: EE00

The selection process involves four review stages:

1. First, a cadre of undergraduate science education majors searches the World Wide Web for interesting science resources. The undergraduates submit about 500 sites a week for consideration.

2. Next, packets of these Web pages are organized and sent to teacher-Webwatchers with expertise in given fields and grade levels. The teacher-Webwatchers can also submit Web pages that they have found on their own. The teachers pick the jewels from this selection and correlate them to the National Science Education Standards. These pages are submitted to the *sci*LINKS database.

3. Scientists review these correlated sites for accuracy.

4. Finally, NSTA staff approve the Web pages and edit the information provided for accuracy and consistent style.

Who pays for *sci*LINKS? *sci*LINKS is a free service for textbook and supplemental resource users, but obviously someone must pay for it. Participating publishers pay a fee to the National Science Teachers Association for each book that contains *sci*LINKS. The program is also supported by a grant from the National Aeronautics and Space Administration (NASA).

GALÁPAGOS:
FRAME OF REFERENCE
CHAPTER 1

WHERE IN THE WORLD?

TEACHER SECTION

This activity is modified from a version created by NSTA for the Smithsonian Institution for the film *Galápagos in 3D*. An online adaptation of this activity can be found at http://pubs.nsta.org/galapagos/.

Background Information

The Galápagos Archipelago, or island group, consists of 13 large islands, six smaller islands, and a great number of small volcanic islets or *rocca*. These islands in the eastern Pacific Ocean are approximately 960 km west of mainland Ecuador in South America, situated along the equator. They lie almost directly south of Chicago, Illinois, in the United States. The geographic position and isolation of the Galápagos are the key to the island group's natural history. To understand why the Galápagos Archipelago is famous as a laboratory of evolution and adaptation, first it is necessary to understand a little about the relationship of life forms to location. Your students will learn how *absolute* location of the islands compares with *relative* location, and will discover how isolated are the Galápagos Islands from the rest of the world.

Aboard the HMS *Beagle*, Charles Darwin traveled west from the coast of South America, exploring the waters of the Galápagos Islands from September 15 through October 20, 1835. Darwin landed on at least six of the larger islands, starting at the island now called San Cristóbal on September 17, 1835 and ending at Pinta Island. The *Beagle* left the Galápagos and sailed toward Tahiti on October 20.

Procedure

Part A

As a class, locate the Galápagos Islands on a globe and measure the distance to the coast of Ecuador using a piece of string. Now take that same piece of string and place one end on your hometown, and find a city that is the same distance from you as the Galápagos are from the mainland.

Distribute to each student a photocopy of a local or regional road map and the student handout *Absolute and Relative Location*, and have them each locate a city of their choice, approximately 900–1,000 km from their hometown. You can let students use this same city in later activities when

Objectives

- To learn basic mapping skills, and to understand the difference between absolute and relative location.

- To understand the importance of careful observations, and to make a permanent record of observations.

- To gain a sense of the history of discovery about how evolution works.

Materials

- Student handouts:

    Absolute and Relative Location

    Map of the Eastern Pacific

    Map of the Galápagos Islands

    Adventuring in the Archipelago: Excerpts from Darwin's Journal

    Adventuring in Your Own Backyard

    Dr. Betsy Jackson's Journal

- Globe

- Copies of a regional or national map

- Local map with latitude and longitude

- String

- Straight edge or ruler

- Pencil

- Notebook or diary

ACTIVITY 1: WHERE IN THE WORLD?

TEACHER SECTION

Topic: longitude/latitude

Go to: www.scilinks.org

Code: EE04

researching climate and local ecology. Students should determine the absolute location of their hometown and other familiar locations on a map that shows latitude and longitude. For example, if you live in Milwaukee, Wisconsin, you can choose Washington, DC, as your comparison city—it is the same distance away as the Galápagos are from Ecuador. The absolute location of Milwaukee is approximately N 43°, W 88°. Your students could describe the relative location of Milwaukee as approximately 1,000 km northwest of Washington or 125 km almost due north of Chicago.

After completing the worksheet, discuss with your students how they think animals and plants located in the other city would get to yours. Point out any significant land barriers, such as bodies of water or mountains, which may hinder such traveling. If no such natural barriers exist, ask students to imagine the two cities are separated by water, and the plants and animals don't swim. The colonization process will be addressed in the *Ecology and Islands* chapter, but this activity will get your students thinking about these questions.

After completing this exercise, students should know where the Galápagos Islands are located, and they should understand the islands' location in both absolute and relative terms.

Part B

This section of the activity will reinforce student understanding of relative geography and will introduce students to the role of journal keeping. Students will follow Darwin's Galápagos adventures by marking some of the locations where he made journal entries while visiting the archipelago.

Divide students into pairs and give to each pair copies of the *Map of the Galápagos Islands* and *Adventuring in the Archipelago: Excerpts from Darwin's Journal*. Each site is introduced by a short quote from Darwin's journals or from *The Voyage of the Beagle*. The absolute positions (latitude and longitude) are listed after each quote. The students should read the quote, note the absolute position, and find the site on the map of the Galápagos Islands. When students find the site they should mark it with a small dot and list the date of the quote. As an option, students can calculate the kilometers between stops and add those to the map.

When all sites have been located, students should "connect the dots" of Darwin's voyage around the Galápagos. As an evaluation of this activity, the students can discuss this part of Darwin's journey or create a journal as though they had accompanied Darwin on his trip.

Part C

To understand the importance of recording observations, ask students to keep their own *Fieldwork Journal*. You can limit the students' keeping a journal to their study of evolution, or it can be continued throughout the term. They can observe and make entries in any kind of notebook, but a hard-cover binder or a permanently bound notebook may help them to take the assignment seriously and encourage them to continue making journal entries after this activity is over.

Distribute the handouts *Adventuring in Your Own Backyard* and *Dr. Betsy Jackson's Journal*. Use the former to guide students in setting up their journal. The second handout introduces students to Dr. Jackson, a fictional character who recurs throughout this book. Through her journal entries, students will be provided with information for use in certain activities. In this section, Dr. Jackson's completed journal entry can serve as an example from which students can model their own journals.

You can structure this activity in a number of ways. One option is to direct where your students observe, e.g., in their own backyard or at a school site. Or, ask them to record their journey to and from school for a few days. Another alternative is to localize their observations to a small model ecosystem in a jar. Students can add a small amount of gravel, pond water, aquarium plants, and a snail to a one-quart jar, seal it, and place it in low light. They can start an *Aquatic Ecosystem Journal* as though they were naturalists who discovered this habitat while on their own "voyage" of discovery. Encourage the students to draw pictures or "field sketches" to help illustrate and add detail to their observations. They can share these observations with the rest of the class at weekly intervals to encourage continued participation.

Develop a set of goals for students in the form of a rubric. Rubrics will vary depending on the structure you choose for each activity; share these goals with students at the start of each section. Check student journals against the rubric at regular, announced intervals throughout the unit or term.

TEACHER SECTION

Standards

The material promoted in this activity enhances and supports student understanding of the following *National Science Education Standards* for grades 5–8:

Populations and Ecosystems (Life Science)

A population consists of all individuals of a species that occur together at a given place and time. All populations living together and the physical factors with which they interact compose an ecosystem.

Science and Technology in Society (History and Nature of Science)

Science and technology have advanced through contributions of many different people, in different cultures, at different times in history. Science and technology have contributed enormously to economic growth and productivity among societies and groups within societies.

Scientists and engineers work in many different settings, including colleges and universities, businesses and industries, specific research institutes, and government agencies.

Science as a Human Endeavor (History and Nature of Science)

Women and men of various social and ethnic backgrounds—and with diverse interests, talents, qualities, and motivations—engage in the activities of science, engineering, and related fields such as the health professions. Some scientists work in teams, and some work alone, but all communicate extensively with others.

Science requires different abilities, depending on such factors as the field of study and type of inquiry. Science is very much a human endeavor, and the work of science relies on basic human qualities, such as reasoning, insight, energy, skill, and creativity—as well as on scientific habits of mind, such as intellectual honesty, tolerance of ambiguity, skepticism, and openness to new ideas.

Nature of Science (History and Nature of Science)

Scientists formulate and test their explanations of nature using observation, experiments, and theoretical and mathematical models. Although all scientific ideas are tentative and subject to change and improvement in principle, for most major ideas in science, there is much experimental and observational confirmation. Those ideas are not likely to change greatly in the future. Scientists change their ideas about nature when they encounter new experimental evidence that does not match their existing explanations.

History of Science (History and Nature of Science)

Many individuals have contributed to the traditions of science. Studying some of these individuals provides further understanding of scientific inquiry, science as a human endeavor, the nature of science, and the relationships between science and society.

In historical perspective, science has been practiced by different individuals in different cultures. In looking at the history of many peoples, one finds that scientists and engineers of high achievement are considered to be among the most valued contributors to their culture.

Assessment

Activity	Exemplary	Emergent	Deficient
Part A	Students are able to describe the differences between absolute and relative location of their own hometown. They will be able to locate the Galápagos Islands on a map or globe. They can explain latitude and longitude.	Students are able to describe the absolute location of their hometown, but do not grasp relative directions. They have an idea where the Galápagos Islands are. They can explain latitude and longitude.	Students cannot describe relative location. They have great difficulty finding the Galápagos Islands on a globe or a map. They do not understand latitude and longitude.
Part B	Students correctly trace Darwin's journey, and write a series of journal entries written as though they were with Darwin, or describe a similar journey.	Students correctly trace Darwin's journey, but cannot relate to the real journey. They have a difficult time describing this kind of journey.	Students have difficulty locating Darwin's landing sites or areas he visited. They cannot describe a similar journey.
Part C	Students keep a journal regularly and include observations of sightings. They describe their journal entries to their classmates during weekly review sessions.	Students keep a journal irregularly. They sometimes include illustrations. Their descriptions of observations are sketchy.	Students often forget to make journal entries. Journal entries are very brief and have few real observations.

ABSOLUTE AND RELATIVE LOCATION

Your teacher will give you copies of a local, regional map and a map of the eastern Pacific Ocean. On your local map, find a city that is the same distance from your hometown as the Galápagos Islands are from mainland Ecuador. You may have to convert between the different scales on the maps.

1. What is the *absolute* location of your hometown and of the city you selected? (Hint: The answers are in latitude and longitude.)

2. Describe the city in *relative* terms in relation to your hometown.

3. How would plants and animals get from this city to your hometown? What barriers—such as mountains or rivers—would they have to cross?

4. What is the *absolute* location of the Galápagos Islands? What is the *relative* location of the islands in relation to mainland Ecuador? What are some ways plants and animals from Ecuador might get to the Galápagos?

MAP OF THE EASTERN PACIFIC

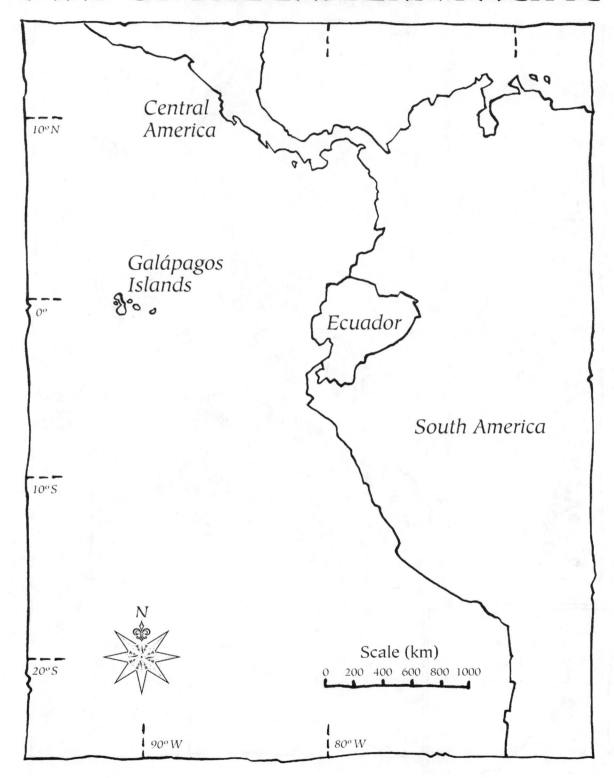

Central
America

10°N

Galápagos
Islands

0°

Ecuador

South America

10°S

N

Scale (km)

0   200 400 600 800 1000

20°S

90°W   80°W

MAP OF THE GALÁPAGOS ISLANDS

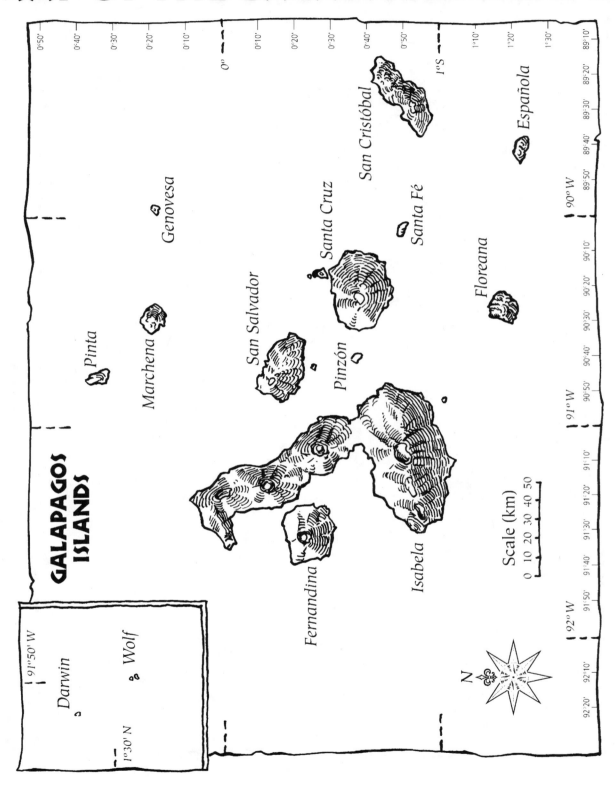

ADVENTURING IN THE ARCHIPELAGO: EXCERPTS FROM DARWIN'S JOURNAL

Now that you know where the Galápagos Islands are located, you are going to travel around this island group and get a feeling for what Charles Darwin found when he visited the islands.

Darwin, aboard the HMS *Beagle*, traveled west from the coast of South America in September 1835, and arrived in the waters of the Galápagos Islands on September 15.

Below are some entries from Darwin's journal, with his absolute position (defined by latitude and longitude) following each entry. On the map your teacher has given you, make a small dot for the location of each quote, and write the date of the quote next to it.

Degrees are written as " ° " and minutes as " ′ " and 1° equals 60′. The equator is 0° latitude, anything located above the equator is north, and anything below the equator is south.

After you have made a dot for each quote, play "connect the dots," starting with the first one, and connect them in order. You will see the approximate route Darwin took during his five weeks of exploration in the Galápagos Islands more than 160 years ago!

Note: When Darwin wrote his journal, he referred to the islands by their English names. Because the islands are part of Ecuador, the names have been changed in Darwin's quotes to reflect the modern Spanish names (the names Darwin used are in parentheses). To avoid confusion, the spelling of certain words has been updated.

EXCERPTS FROM DARWIN'S JOURNAL

September 17, 1835

In the morning we landed on San Cristóbal (Chatham) Island, which, like the others, rises with a tame and rounded outline, broken here and there by scattered hillocks, the remains of former craters. Nothing could be less inviting than the first appearance. A broken field of black basaltic lava, thrown into the most rugged waves, and crossed by great fissures, is everywhere covered by stunted, sunburned brushwood, which shows little signs of life.

Location: 0°47´ S, 89°30´ W

September 19–22, 1835

The Beagle sailed round San Cristóbal (Chatham), and anchored in several bays. One night I slept on shore on a part of the island, where black truncated cones [volcanoes] were extraordinarily numerous: from one small eminence I counted sixty of them, all surmounted by craters more or less perfect. As I was walking along I met two large tortoises, each of which must have weighed at least two hundred pounds: one was eating a piece of cactus, and as I approached, it stared at me and slowly walked away; the other gave a deep hiss, and drew in its head.

Location: 1° S, 89°30´ W

September 23, 1835

The Beagle proceeded to Floreana (Charles) Island. This archipelago has long been frequented, first by the buccaneers, and latterly by whalers, but it is only within the last six years, that a small colony has been established here. The inhabitants are between two and three hundred in number; they are nearly all people of color, who have been banished for political crimes from the Republic of Ecuador, of which Quito is the capital.

Location: 1°15´ S, 90°20´ W

September 29, 1835

We doubled the south-west extremity of Isabela (Albermarle) Island, and the next day were nearly becalmed between it and Fernandina Island. Both are covered with immense deluges of black naked lava, which have flowed either over the rims of the great caldrons, like pitch over the rim of a pot in which it has been boiled, or have burst forth from smaller orifices on the flanks; in their descent they have spread over miles of the sea-coast. On both of these islands, eruptions are known to have taken place; and in Isabela, we saw a small jet of smoke curling from the summit of one of the great craters.

Location: 0°17´ S, 91°23´ W

EXCERPTS FROM DARWIN'S JOURNAL

October 3, 1835

We sailed around the northern end of Isabela (Albermarle) Island. Nearly the whole of this side is covered with recent streams of dark-colored lavas, and is studded with craters. I should think it would be difficult to find in any other part of the world, an island situated within the tropics, and of such considerable size (namely 75 miles [120 km] long,) so sterile and incapable of supporting life.

Location: 0º10´ N, 91º20´ W

October 8, 1835

We arrived at San Salvador (James) Island. Mr. Bynoe, myself, and our servants were left here for a week, with provisions and a tent, whilst the Beagle *went for water. We found here a party of Spaniards, who had been sent from Floreana (Charles) Island to dry fish, and to salt tortoise-meat.*

Location: 0º10´ S, 90º50´ W

October 18, 1835

Finished survey of Isabela (Albermarle) Island.

Location: 0º7´ S, 91º15´ W

October 19, 1835

To Pinta (Abingdon) Island.

Location: 0º32´ N, 90º45´ W

October 19, 1835

Darwin and Wolf Islands.

Location: 1º30´ N, 91º50´ W

October 20, 1835

The survey of the Galápagos Archipelago being concluded, we steered towards Tahiti and commenced our long passage of 3,200 miles [5,120 km]. In the course of a few days we sailed out of the gloomy and clouded ocean-district which extends during the winter far from the coast of South America. We then enjoyed bright and clear weather, while running pleasantly along at the rate of 150 or 160 miles [240–256 km] a day before the steady trade-wind. The temperature in this more central part of the Pacific is higher than near the American shore.

Location: 17º37´ S, 149º27´ W *(off the map)*

ADVENTURING IN YOUR OWN BACKYARD

Keeping a journal is a crucial part of any fieldwork. Explorers and scientists keep journals of their investigations and adventures. Scientists keep journals to provide a permanent record of what they witness in the natural world—like a diary of nature. When scientists look back at pages from weeks gone by, they will know the exact day they saw a particular animal or other natural phenomena. If you keep a journal of your observations in the same area for several years, you will begin to notice patterns; eventually you'll be able to predict when certain animals will return to the area or when particular plants will bloom.

"This volume contains, in the form of a journal, a history of our voyage, and a sketch of those observations in Natural History and Geology." Thus begins *The Voyage Of the Beagle*, the journal Charles Darwin kept on his voyages. Throughout his life Darwin kept many volumes of journals from his observations and studies of nature. He carried a small notebook wherever he went, and later transferred his notes to the master journal that was kept on board the *Beagle*.

Like Darwin, you are a field scientist studying a newly discovered habitat. To help you remember what you observe, you will keep a journal. Scientists keep journals of their projects, and they do it for a reason: journals are invaluable for keeping track of, and making sense of, their work.

In your journal you will share your observations about a particular environment you are investigating. You will observe nature and ask *why* or *how* about the things you see. Why is the male cardinal a bright red, but the female a dull brown? Why doesn't a cactus need a lot of water compared to most plants? How can the ant carry a piece of bread several times its size? What, why, how, and where are the overriding questions that scientists ask. You need to think about the things you observe, and your journal is the place to record your observations, questions, and hypotheses (possible explanations for what you observe).

On your first day, select a place to focus upon, and write a detailed description. Use all of your senses—what does it look like, how does it smell, what sounds can you hear? Make sure to include where your place is located (in both absolute and relative terms). For all subsequent entries, make sure to list each date and the time you observed. See if you can find a central theme or idea, such as encountering a bird's nest and then recording the changes with each observation. Make sure to record your observations each time, while your thoughts are fresh. Your teacher will help direct your observations and your journal writing activity.

Much of what we know about the Galápagos Islands of the eighteenth and nineteenth centuries came from journals kept by explorers like Darwin. Remember, to be a good scientist you must be curious and you must observe the world around you—and you must record what you see in your field journal.

DR. BETSY JACKSON'S JOURNAL

Below is a journal entry from Dr. Betsy Jackson, an ecologist working as a field researcher at the Darwin Research Station in the Galápagos Islands. She arrived in the islands in February 1999 to research the Galápagos giant tortoise, *Geochelone elephantopus*. Dr. Jackson's journal describes her observations and experiences in the Galápagos, just as does Darwin's journal. Here is a sample of one of the journal entries she made soon after arriving at the Galápagos Islands.

February 12, 1999

The weather is quite different from my native Ohio. February in Ohio is usually very cold and often snowy, whereas here on the equator it is hot. There is a light rain today, but the temperature is almost 27° C. It is an incredible coincidence that I should arrive in the Galápagos on Darwin's birthday. He was born February 12, 1809; he would have been 190 years old today!

I am at the Darwin Research Station on Santa Cruz Island now. I am getting settled in and will soon travel to Española Island and begin my studies on the giant tortoise and other animals that are a part of the tortoise ecosystem, such as the marine iguana and the famous Darwin finches. Although Santa Cruz is one of the islands with a large human population, it is still a great place to observe nature. The highlands are interesting because the climate is quite different from the desert-like environment around the research station. I am looking forward to exploring all the diverse mini-ecosystems on Santa Cruz.

I arrived on Santa Cruz after flying into the airport on Baltra Island. The ride from the northern side of the island was exciting. We drove through many different environments as we climbed through the highlands and then traveled back down to the arid region to the town of Puerto Ayora. Puerto Ayora is one of the largest towns in the Galápagos. My first impression of the Darwin Research Station was how dry it is. I saw shruby trees and cactus growing in dry, sandy soil and noticed a number of the famous small birds that Darwin described in his journals. These finches are rather drab and very difficult to distinguish from one another. I have read about Darwin's finches, and here I was observing them flying from bush to cactus to the plants growing along the road.

As I walked from the town to the research station I saw a number of small buildings that housed both the administrative offices and the laboratories of the station. Just past the labs I came upon three tortoise pens in a visitor center, operated by the Galápagos National Park. The tortoises in these pens are studied by the scientists at the Darwin Station, but cannot be used for breeding purposes because scientists do not know what island they originally came from. Visitors are allowed to get very close to these giants, but they cannot touch them or get in the way of their feeding area. I sat and watched two male tortoises exhibiting a "posturing behavior" by standing and stretching their necks to the sky while facing one another. They stood with their mouths wide open. It almost seemed like one was waiting for the other one to back down.

DR. BETSY JACKSON'S JOURNAL

It was getting late and I still had not checked in at the office of the research station, but I had one more stop I wanted to make. The Galápagos National Park, along with the research station, has set up a "Tortoise Rearing Station." The park wardens collect tortoise eggs from the wild and bring them here. The eggs are endangered in the wild because introduced animals that are not native to the islands (such as dogs or goats) will eat them. So, the eggs are collected, marked, and brought to the research station. I also had the fun of seeing young tortoises that were only one- or two-years old scrambling towards dinner—large bunches of vegetation provided by their human caretakers. It is hard to believe a small animal less than 10 cm across will someday grow into a giant tortoise weighing more than 11 kilos (400 pounds)! Each young tortoise has an identification number painted on its shell so the scientists can study it and be able to identify which island it came from so it can be released when it is big enough to defend itself from the introduced animal predators.

This afternoon I am going to observe the most famous Galápagos tortoise of them all—Lonesome George. George is a visitor at the Research Station because he is being studied. He is thought to be the very last tortoise of the subspecies that inhabited Pinta Island to the north. Just think, the very last one alive. Sad!! But I guess that is one of the reasons I am going to study the giant tortoise—to find out if they are in danger of extinction and just what can be done about it. Well George, I'm excited to finally meet you!!!

TORTOISE'S LONG DISTANCE CALL

The Washington Post, November 15, 1999.

The Galápagos Islands off the coast of Ecuador helped inspire Charles Darwin's renowned theory of evolution.

Lonesome George

The islands are home to some of the world's most exotic creatures, including the giant Galápagos tortoise, which can grow up to 5 feet long and weight up to 650 pounds, making it the world's largest living tortoise.

Only one male of one subspecies of the tortoise remains alive today.

Conservation scientists have been trying to mate him with females from the islands closest to his to keep the subspecies alive. But "Lonesome George" has never shown any interest. Now, researchers think they know why.

An international team of scientists from Yale University in New Haven, Conn., the State University of New York in Syracuse, and the University of Rome in Italy analyzed the genes of tortoise species around the world. To their surprise, the researchers found that George is more closely related to tortoises found on the islands of Española and San Cristóbal, which are farthest from George's original home island of Pinta.

"This finding may provide guidance in finding a mate for Lonesome George, who so far has failed to reproduce," the researchers wrote in the Nov. 9 issue of the *Proceedings of the National Academy*.

THINKING IN TIME SCALES

Background Information

Students have a difficult time comprehending how short the span of human history is in relation to Earth's geological history. In the next activity, *Reports from the Galápagos*, students will learn about the role the Galápagos Islands have played in recent human history. There, they will work with time scales ranging from the earliest written descriptions of the islands to the present. This activity will help students visualize these varying scales of time, and create a mental picture of time in terms of millions and billions of years. The immense span of time allows geologic forces to "set the stage" for the ecological development of an area. On this stage plays the development, survival, and evolution of species that live there. This activity relies on basic mathematics skills, and students will need to switch between thinking about thousands of years to thinking about billions of years, so you may wish to review mathematics concepts before you begin.

Ask the students to tell you what they mean when they say that something happened "a long time ago." (Answers will range from a few months to centuries and beyond.) Ask them to list events that occurred a long time ago. Record these events without comment. Emphasize that scientists seek proof of how long ago events occurred by studying things that record the passage of long periods of time, such as the layers in rocks (strata) and index fossils. A large number of strata indicates a long time period of deposition. The presence of index fossils—fossils of species that existed only during specific time periods—provide an index to the age of rocks. Radiometric dating techniques can also reveal how long ago rocks were formed. The dating of events that occurred a long time ago and the sequence in which they occurred are among the puzzles scientists must solve. We are constantly adding to our knowledge of Earth's history.

Procedure

Obtain 12 reams of standard-size paper and stack them on the floor or on a desk where they will be visible to all the students. Unwrap only the top ream.

Objectives

- To develop a mental picture of the time period of their own lives, the period of human history, and the age of Earth and events in Earth history.

- To connect mathematics, geology, and recent human history by working with changing time scales.

Materials

- Student handouts:

    2,000 Dots

    Twenty Centuries

    Selected Events in Human History & Geologic Time Scale

    Earth History Events (one per class, cut into strips along the dotted lines)

- Twelve, 500-sheet reams of 8½" x 11" paper

- Pencils

ACTIVITY 2: THINKING IN TIME SCALES

TEACHER SECTION

On each of the lower reams, tear a strip 7- to 10-cm wide from the side of each wrapper so the paper shows through. The result should be a column of exposed paper edges (to show the stratification, or layers, of paper). Stack the unwrapped twelfth ream neatly on top (see illustration at left). Inform students that every page in the stack stands for the same period of time, and the stack is 12 reams high.

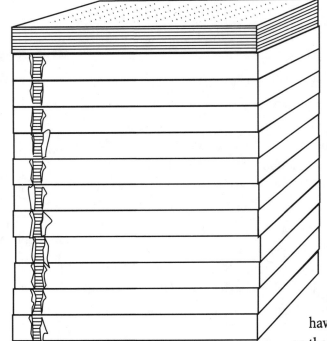

12 reams of paper, top ream unwrapped

2,000 Dots worksheet on top

tears in each ream wrapper, exposing layers of paper

Before class you should cut into strips the *Earth History Events* worksheet. Put the strips into a box and let each student blindly choose one. There are 24 events, so you will need to budget the strips based on the number of students in your class. Then distribute the rest of the student handouts, one per student, and have students answer the questions on the *Twenty Centuries* worksheet. This worksheet will help them visualize different time scales, one for recent history, one for geological events. An extended discussion of the *Geologic Time Scale* may be appropriate.

Answers to student questions:

1. At the top of the 2,000 Dots *sheet, write the words "Twenty Centuries." This sheet has 2,000 dots; each dot = 1 year. Show how 2,000 years equals 20 centuries.*

2,000 years divided by 100 years in a century = 20 centuries.

Steps 2. and 3. are procedural and do not require answers.

4. Look at the Geologic Time Scale. *Where do these events, and even the oldest dot on the worksheet, fit on this chart?*

They do not because the scale is too large to fit these events.

TEACHER SECTION

5. At the front of the room is a stack of 12 reams of paper, each of which has 500 sheets. If each sheet has 2,000 dots (each representing 1 year), how many years are represented by the entire stack of paper?

> 2,000 dots per page at 1 year per dot x 500 sheets of paper per ream x 12 reams of paper = 12,000,000 years (12 million years, with each sheet of paper representing 2,000 years)

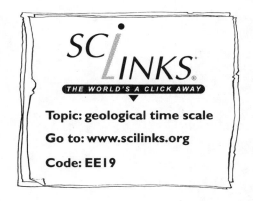

Topic: geological time scale

Go to: www.scilinks.org

Code: EE19

6. Now, cross out the words "Twenty Centuries" at the top of the page, and write "Two Thousand Centuries." Instead of each dot = 1 year, now each dot = 100 years (one century). Look at the stack of 12 reams of paper again. If each sheet has 2,000 dots (each representing 100 years), how many years are now represented by the entire stack of paper?

> 2,000 dots per page at 100 years per dot x 500 sheets of paper per ream x 12 reams of paper = 1,200,000,000 years (1.2 billion years, with each sheet of paper representing 200,000 years)

7. Look at your strip of paper with a geologic event written on it, and mark on the Geologic Time Scale when the event occurred. Will this event fit within the span of years represented by the stack of paper? If so, calculate how far down in the paper stack to place your individual marker, then come forward to place it at the correct depth. If not, use the mathematics you have already done to calculate how much more paper would be needed, and share your results with the class.

> The entire stack represents 1,200,000,000 (1.2 billion) years. Some of the events on the strips of paper will fit within the reams (e.g., 1 million years ago will be 5 sheets from the top, .5 billion years will be 5 reams from the top). Some of the events are older than 1.2 billion years, so students will need to do additional calculations to figure out the number of reams of paper needed. You may want to have these students write their answers on the board, because they were not able to put their strip in the stack of papers at the front of the class.

Additional discussion suggestions:

Earth is approximately 4.6 billion years old. How many reams of paper like the ones in the front of the classroom would it take to represent that many years?

> Forty-six reams, almost four times as much as is presently there.

ACTIVITY 2: THINKING IN TIME SCALES

TEACHER SECTION

Now that you have an idea of the age of Earth, would you describe the Galápagos Islands as young or old?

> They are relatively young, less than five million years for the oldest islands. As volcanic eruptions presently occur, the islands are still forming.

Compare these answers with the students' earlier guesses. Emphasize that terms like *young and old, long ago,* and *recent* can have very different meanings in different contexts (e.g., our lifetime, written history, human history, geologic time).

Standards

The material promoted in this activity enhances and supports student understanding of the following *National Science Education Standards* for grades 5–8:

Structure of Earth System (Earth and Space Science)

> The solid Earth is layered with a lithosphere; hot, convecting mantle; and dense, metallic core.

> Land forms are the result of a combination of constructive and destructive forces. Constructive forces include crustal deformation, volcanic eruption, and deposition of sediment, while destructive forces include weathering and erosion.

> Some changes in the solid Earth can be described as the *rock cycle.* Old rocks at Earth's surface weather, forming sediments that are buried, then compacted, heated, and often recrystallized into new rock. Eventually, those new rocks may be brought to the surface by the forces that drive plate motions, and the rock cycle continues.

> Soil consists of weathered rocks and decomposed organic material from dead plants, animals, and bacteria. Soils are often found in layers, with each having a different chemical composition and texture.

Earth's History (Earth and Space Science)

> The Earth processes we see today, including erosion, movement of lithospheric plates, and changes in atmospheric composition, are similar to those that occurred in the past. Earth history is also influenced by occasional catastrophes, such as the impact of an asteroid or comet.

> Fossils provide important evidence of how life and environmental conditions have changed.

Assessment

Activity	Exemplary	Emergent	Deficient
	Students are able to accurately place their "event" into the stack of paper. They can calculate how much paper is needed to accurately model the age of Earth. Students accurately describe the age of the Galápagos Islands and explain that dinosaurs came before humans.	Students can find the correct location of their event, but have some difficulty calculating how much paper is necessary to represent the age of Earth. Students have a good idea of the age of the Galápagos Islands and know that dinosaurs preceded humans.	Students have a difficult time finding where their event should be placed in the stack of paper. Students cannot calculate how much paper is needed to show Earth's age. The age of the Galápagos is also not understood. They may know that dinosaurs preceded humans.

2,000 DOTS

TWENTY CENTURIES

For this activity, you should have two handouts: *2,000 Dots* and *Selected Events in Human History* & *Geologic Time Scale*, and a strip of paper that has some geologic event written on it. Every dot on the *2,000 Dots* sheet represents one year, the last dot on the bottom line is this year, each dot before that one is a previous year. Follow the directions below and answer the questions on a separate sheet of paper.

1. At the top of the *2,000 Dots* sheet, write the words "Twenty Centuries." This sheet has 2,000 dots; each dot = 1 year. Show how 2,000 years equals 20 centuries.

2. The first dot at the top of the line represents the year 2000; each dot after that is a previous year. Draw a circle around the year you were born, and write the year next to that dot. Now draw a circle around the year one of your parents was born. Then draw a circle around the year one of your grandparents was born (estimate if necessary). Write the years next to the dots. You've now placed the time frame for three generations of your family on the page.

3. For each event listed on the *Selected Events in Human History* worksheet, circle the appropriate dot on the *2,000 Dots* sheet, and write the year next to that dot.

4. Look at the *Geologic Time Scale*. Where do these events, and even the oldest dot on the worksheet, fit on this chart?

5. At the front of the room is a stack of 12 reams of paper, each of which has 500 sheets. If each sheet has 2,000 dots (each representing 1 year), how many years are represented by the entire stack of paper?

6. Now, cross out the words "Twenty Centuries" at the top of the page, and write "Two Thousand Centuries." Instead of each dot = 1 year, now each dot = 100 years (one century). Look at the stack of 12 reams of paper again. If each sheet has 2,000 dots (each representing 100 years), how many years are now represented by the entire stack of paper?

7. Look at your strip of paper with a geologic event written on it, and mark on the *Geologic Time Scale* when the event occurred. Will this event fit within the span of years represented by the stack of paper? If so, calculate how far down in the paper stack to place your individual marker, then come forward to place it at the correct depth. If not, use the mathematics you have already done to calculate how much more paper would be needed, and share your results with the class.

SELECTED EVENTS IN HUMAN HISTORY

1776 .... U.S. Congress adopts the Declaration of Independence.

1912 .... Wright Brothers launch their first successful flight.

1492 .... Columbus reaches the Americas.

1904 .... Henry Ford markets the automobile.

1835 .... Darwin visits the Galápagos.

1959 .... The Galápagos Islands are given National Park status, and the Darwin Foundation is formed.

_____ .... My great-grandmother is born. (Estimate.)

1200 .... The Incan Empire (later to include Ecuador) begins its rise.

1564 .... William Shakespeare is born.

1969 .... Humans first walk on the moon.

GEOLOGIC TIME SCALE

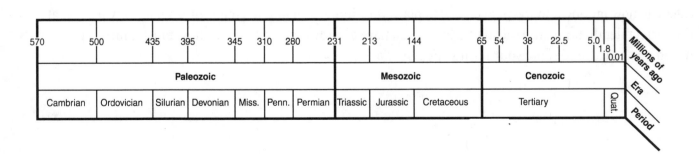

EARTH HISTORY EVENTS

Earth formed: 4,600,000,000 years ago

North and South America joined by the closing of the Panama Isthmus: 2,800,000 years ago

Earliest known hominid (human ancestor) fossils deposited: 4,400,000 years ago

Earliest known Galápagos rocks formed: 4,000,000 years ago

Earliest known animal fossils (jellyfish-like organisms) deposited: 1,200,000,000 years ago

Earliest known fish fossils deposited: 500,000,000 years ago

Earliest known reptile fossils deposited: 290,000,000 years ago

Earliest known bird fossils deposited: 160,000,000 years ago

Earliest known mammal fossils deposited: 200,000,000 years ago

Earliest known flowering plant fossils deposited: 135,000,000 years ago

Earliest known trilobite fossils deposited: 600,000,000 years ago

Appalachian Mountains formed: 250,000,000 years ago

Rocky Mountains formed: 70,000,000 years ago

Mass extinction of dinosaurs: 65,000,000 years ago

Breakup of Pangaea began: 180,000,000 years ago

Earliest known fossils of land animals deposited: 390,000,000 years ago

Last Ice Age ended: 10,000 years ago

Oldest known rock on Earth formed in southwest Greenland: 3,200,000,000 years ago

Alps and Himalayas begin forming as India joined Asian continent: 30,000,000 years ago

Formation of iron, copper, and nickel ores: 1,000,000,000 years ago

Much of continental land masses underwater: 330,000,000 years ago

Active volcanoes in New England: 210,000,000 years ago

Earliest microfossils formed in South African chert: 3,200,000,000 years ago

Algae deposited in Rhodesian limestones: 3,000,000,000 years ago

*All dates are approximate, and these events actually occurred over a range of time.

REPORTS FROM THE GALÁPAGOS

TEACHER SECTION

This activity is modified from a version created by NSTA for the Smithsonian Institution for the film *Galapagos in 3D*. An online adaptation of this activity can be found at http://pubs.nsta.org/galapagos/.

Background Information

In the previous activity students learned about the Galápagos in the geological time scale of millions and billions of years. Now they should focus on a historical time scale of hundreds of years, for which there are written records. Although the Galápagos Islands were "discovered" by western explorers five hundred years ago—and probably explored by South American native populations before that—only recently have people taken up permanent residence there. Before these settlements arose, people were only occasional visitors to these remote islands. The array of temporary Galápagos residents has included such colorful characters as shipwrecked explorers, pirates, whalers, prisoners, scientists, and vagabonds looking for fortunes.

In this activity, students will read letters, journal entries, and other written descriptions by visitors to the Galápagos between 1535 and the present. Scientists keep journals as careful records of their observations, so weeks or years later they know the exact day they saw a strange animal or had a particular idea. Explorers often used diaries to keep track of their travels. Notes about landmarks or settlements could prove crucial when traveling in unknown waters. Even letters to friends and family help provide a snapshot of what life was like in earlier times. The letters and journals in the student handout *Letters from the Galápagos* are based on the observations of actual visitors to the Galápagos over a period of 465 years. Most are taken from original sources. Although the letters from the settler and the World War II nurse are fictional, the events they describe are real.

Note: When many of these letters were written, the islands were referred to by their English names. Because the islands are part of Ecuador, the names have been changed to reflect the modern Spanish names. To avoid confusion, the spelling of certain words has been updated.

Objectives

- To investigate how the Galápagos have been affected by human visitors from different historical periods, from 1535 to the present.

- To create a timeline of important events in the history of the Galápagos from a chronology that is provided.

Materials

- Student handouts:

    Letters from the Galápagos

    Selected Events in History
    (cut up into squares)

- Tape or glue

- Colored pencils

- Sheets of 8½" x 14" legal-size paper (at least five per group)

ACTIVITY 3: REPORTS FROM THE GALÁPAGOS

TEACHER SECTION

Procedure

Part A

Divide the class into groups of four or eight; distribute copies of the handout *Letters from the Galápagos*. With your class in groups of four, each student will be responsible for two letters; if in groups of eight, each student will have one letter.

Have the students compose a reply letter to their author, interviewing them about the Galápagos scene they described. Student questions should indicate that they understood the original letter. Students can also role-play the parts of the author, or contemporary interviewer, or act out a short skit that portrays the scene described in each letter.

Another option is to ask each student to illustrate the scene described in his or her letter. Students may need to be creative to illustrate some of the described scenes.

Part B

Before class, make copies of the student handout *Selected Events in History* (one for each group). Cut up the squares before class and shuffle the squares so they are not in order. Make sure each group has all of the squares in the chronology. You can also let your students do the cutting and mixing as their abilities allow, to promote a sense of interest in the project.

During class, have the groups of students create a timeline by taping together five sheets of 8½" x 14" paper, with the short sides taped together. Each sheet will represent one century. Ask the students to mark the timeline by year, in increments of 10 years, starting with the year 1500 (for example, the first sheet will have 1500, 1510, 1520, etc., marked along the line). Have students tape or glue the event squares onto the correct century page, and draw a line from the square to the appropriate spot on the timeline. Colored pencils will help the students better keep track of the lines. You may want to have the students put the cards in order before they begin to tape them to the timeline, to be sure they allow enough space.

After the timeline has been filled in, have the students tape their letter(s) in the appropriate space on the timeline.

Standards

The material promoted in this activity enhances and supports student understanding of the following *National Science Education Standards* for grades 5–8:

Science as a Human Endeavor (History and Nature of Science)

Women and men of various social and ethnic backgrounds—and with diverse interests, talents, qualities, and motivations—engage in the activities of science, engineering, and related fields such as the health professions. Some scientists work in teams, and some work alone, but all communicate extensively with others.

Science requires different abilities, depending on such factors as the field of study and type of inquiry. Science is very much a human endeavor, and the work of science relies on basic human qualities, such as reasoning, insight, energy, skill, and creativity—as well as on scientific habits of mind, such as intellectual honesty, tolerance of ambiguity, skepticism, and openness to new ideas.

History of Science (History and Nature of Science)

Many individuals have contributed to the traditions of science. Studying some of these individuals provides further understanding of scientific inquiry, science as a human endeavor, the nature of science, and the relationships between science and society.

In historical perspective, science has been practiced by different individuals in different cultures. In looking at the history of many peoples, one finds that scientists and engineers of high achievement are considered to be among the most valued contributors to their culture.

Tracing the history of science can show how difficult it was for scientific innovators to break through the accepted ideas of their time to reach the conclusions that we currently take for granted.

TEACHER SECTION
Assessment

Activity	Exemplary	Emergent	Deficient
Part A	Students develop and write a detailed reply to the author of the quote assigned. They include appropriate questions about the Galápagos indicating a familiarity with the original letter. Option: Students create and act in a role-play that indicates an understanding of the original letter.	Students are able to write an original reply, but it lacks detail and does not reflect much information. Option: Students are not able to create a detailed role-play, or it lacks detail.	Students do not compose an original letter, or the letter shows little understanding of or familiarity with the original letter.
Part B	Students create an accurate timeline of the history of the Galápagos Islands and select historical events. They tape the selected events correctly on the timeline.	Students need help creating the timeline and finding where to place events.	Students do not create an accurate timeline or do not place the selected events on it.

LETTERS FROM THE GALÁPAGOS

Fray Tomás de Berlanga

Fray Tomás de Berlanga, spiritual head of all the known and unknown Spanish territories in the Americas, was sent to Peru from 1534 to 1537 by the Pope to investigate conditions under the governorship of the conquistador Francisco Pizarro, especially charges that Native Americans were being treated cruelly. During eight days with no wind, en route to Peru, crew members sighted one of the Galápagos Islands and decided to go ashore for water.

April 5, 1535, Berlanga's report to Charles V, the Holy Roman Emperor

The water on the ship gave out and we were three days in reaching the island on account of the calms, during which all of us, horses as well as people, suffered great hardships. The boat once anchored, ... some were given charge of making a well. From the well there came out water saltier than that of the sea... With the thirst the people felt, they resorted to a leaf of some thistles like prickly pears, and because they were somewhat juicy, although not very tasty, we began to eat of them and squeeze them to draw all the water from them. [Before fresh water was located, on the third day ashore, three men and 10 horses died of thirst.]

On a second island we saw many seals, turtles, iguanas, tortoises, and many birds like those of Spain, but so silly that they do not know how to flee, and many were caught in the hand. On the whole island, I do not think that there is a place where one might sow a bushel of corn. It is as though God had sometime showered stones; and the earth there is worthless, because it has not even the power of raising a little grass.

LETTERS FROM THE GALÁPAGOS

Captain John Cook

In the seventeenth century, Spanish ships carrying wealth from South America were tempting prey for pirates. Pirate Captain John Cook called his ship the *Bachelor's Delight*, and his crew of buccaneers the "Merry Boys." He found the Galápagos, for all their inconveniences, ideal places to hide while waiting for a passing ship.

March 8, 1684, from Cook's journal

We landed at Lobos to mend our caravel [ship] and spy for galleons. After we had been watching for about a week we sighted three tall Spanish treasure ships. Because we had the advantage of surprise, we were able to overpower them easily. We captured 100 prisoners, but when we ransacked their stores we found no [treasure], but only much timber, 1,500 bags of flour, and eight tonnes of quince marmalade. One of the prisoners laughed in our faces and told us that his ship, the flagship of the fleet, had left Lima with 800,000 pieces of eight. When they landed at Guanchoco for water and fresh provisions, however, they heard that our caravel had been sighted, so they left the gold pieces there for safekeeping.

We came to anchor in a very good harbor, lying toward the northernmost end of a fine island under the equinoctial [equator]. This was one of the islands the Spanish call enchanted islands, saying they are but shadows and no real islands. Here being great plenty of provisions, as fish, sea and kind tortoises, some of which weighed at least 200 pound weight, which are excellent good food. We put in at many other islands, but we could find no good water on any of all these, save on the San Salvador Island. Some of the Spanish cargo we left in caves on the islands for another time that we have need.

LETTERS FROM THE GALÁPAGOS

Captain James Colnett

The whaling industry dominated shipping in the 18th century. By the end of that century, so many whales had been killed that they were scarce in the Atlantic. Great Britain's Royal Navy loaned the services of the experienced Captain James Colnett to a whaling company interested in exploring the Pacific. On one of his many voyages around the Galápagos, Colnett may have set up the post office barrel on Santa María Island. To this day visiting ships check the barrel for outbound mail.

1792, from Colnett's journal

I frequently observe the whales coming, as it were, from the main and passing along from the dawn of day until the night in one extended line, as if they were in haste to reach the Galápagos. It is very much to be regretted that these isles have been so little known but only to the Spaniards.

On reaching the South point of San Salvador Isle I got sight of three other islands which I had not seen before. The southernmost island [Santa Fé] is the largest and was the greatest distance from me. ... This isle appears to have been a favorite resort of the buccaneers, as we found not only seats, which had been made by them of earth and stone, but a considerable number of broken jars scattered about... in which the Peruvian wine and liquors of that country are preserved. We also found some old daggers, nails, and other implements.

ACTIVITY 3: REPORTS FROM THE GALÁPAGOS

LETTERS FROM THE GALÁPAGOS

Captain David Porter

During the War of 1812, the United States was the underdog. American strategists looked for indirect ways to harass their opponent—the superior, but overextended, British Navy. One of the most successful of such operations was led by Captain David Porter and based in the Galápagos. With only one ship, the Essex, Porter managed to capture more than half of Great Britain's whaling fleet. Letters intercepted from the post office barrel on Santa María Island helped him to accomplish his mission.

1812, from Porter's report to his superiors

Although we knew from the letters that ships were to be expected, we waited two anxious weeks in the Galápagos before we saw the first sail. The prized [captured] ships were worth our wait, however, containing many provisions of which we stood in great need. We obtained an abundant supply of cordage [rope], canvas, paints, and tar, all of the best quality. We found on board of them also fresh meat to furnish our crew with several delicious meals. They had been in at James [San Salvador] Island, and had supplied themselves abundantly with those extraordinary animals which properly deserve the name of elephant tortoise. The most valuable item of all we captured, however, was water, even though it was contained in the oily casks of the whale-ship, and from them derived no very agreeable taste or smell.

I would advise every vessel visiting the Galápagos to lay in good store of that necessary article, for all the fresh water in the islands owes its existence to temporary rains, and cannot be relied upon. We did however find fresh food to counteract the scurvy, both an herb resembling spinach and other fresh herbs. We found prickly pears in great abundance, stewed them with sugar, and used them to make excellent pies, tarts, etc., which helped to keep the men healthy.

LETTERS FROM THE GALÁPAGOS

Charles Darwin

Charles Darwin spent five weeks in the Galápagos in 1835. What he saw there was to occupy his mind for the rest of his life and influence the thinking of all future generations. His first impression of the islands, like that of most visitors, was rather negative. When his party landed a boat on San Cristóbal Island, the black sand burned their feet right through their shoes.

1835 or later, Darwin's journal notes

The black rocks, heated by the rays of the vertical sun like a stove, give to the air a close and sultry feeling. The plants also smell unpleasantly. The whole country was like we might imagine the cultivated parts of [hell]. The rocks on the beach are frequented by large ... most disgusting clumsy lizards. They are as black as the porous rocks over which they crawl and seek their prey from the sea. Somebody calls them "imps of darkness." They assuredly well become the land they inhabit.

LETTERS FROM THE GALÁPAGOS

Early Galápagos Settler

William Beebe's 1924 book about the islands, *Galapagos, World's End*, was an international bestseller. The idea of living astride the equator was particularly appealing to people in cold northern climates. Many Norwegians responded to an advertising campaign mounted by the unscrupulous Harry Randall, who charged potential emigrants large sums of money to settle in the Galápagos. Within two years of arriving in the Galápagos, all but a handful of the settlers had died or gone home.

1927, from a settler's letter home

As you know, Klaus and I paid Mr. Randall a total of 6,000 kroners, our life savings. Then we borrowed from both our families and sold everything we owned to purchase cows, chickens, seeds, tools, timber, a tractor and fishing equipment. I even sold my wedding ring to buy a drill, since Randall told us there were diamonds to be mined in the islands. After a long and dangerous journey, we landed on Santa María Island. You cannot imagine the scene that met our eyes! There was nothing but hideous, bare, black rock, with grotesque animals, spiny cactuses, and a cold, soaking rain over everything.

The next day we went to work and began building houses, roads, and dams to store water. In the morning the rains came again, and washed everything away. When there is no rain, our stored water leaks out through the cracks in the rock. This is a land that makes people go insane. The only creatures that thrive are the cattle and chickens we brought, and the pigs and dogs that other families brought with them. The animals of the islands are monsters not fit to eat, though they seem not to mind our intrusion. How I long for all of you at home!

LETTERS FROM THE GALÁPAGOS

World War II Nurse

Although World War I had little or no impact on the Galápagos, as World War II approached and the importance of military air power grew, the islands were recognized for their strategic location. In 1938, American President Franklin Roosevelt visited the islands, which were a weak spot for the Panama Canal. In 1942 the U.S. Air Force built a base on Baltra Island (located just north of Santa Cruz), both to shield the Canal and to prevent the islands from being used as a base by the Japanese. The United States abandoned the base in 1947. Afterwards, its materials were recycled into homes all over the Galápagos, and the Ecuadorian Air Force established its own headquarters on the island. Most visitors to the Galápagos now arrive on Baltra, and depart from there.

1942, letter written by an American nurse

> Never has this island heard such noise—at least not since the last time the volcano erupted! Our engineers are using tons of dynamite to blast the lava level enough for an airstrip. For two of them, in fact. Plans call for a pair of landing strips, each 1,800 meters long! There have been some accidents, of course, but nothing worse than the loss of a few fingers. I doubt if any of the hearing loss the crew has suffered will be permanent. Our corps is also building hospitals, such as the one where I will work, roads, and a water distillation plant, so we'll no longer need to fill up our living space with bottled water. I suspect that once the work is done both crew and officers will find this service boring, but perhaps by that time the war will be over. Here, though we keep watch 24 hours a day for Japanese planes, we are so far away from the war that we can almost forget the bloodshed.

LETTERS FROM THE GALÁPAGOS

Dr. Carole Baldwin

The El Niño events are an opportunity for some scientists and a setback for others, just as they were a boon to some species and a disaster for others. The rhythm of nature was thrown off course, and so was the rhythm of work at the Charles Darwin Research Station (CDRS). Life gradually goes back to normal, but after the 1982–83 El Niño there was so little rain that when fires broke out in 1985 there was not enough water to put them out. The CDRS burned that year, along with most of its contents. Fires on Isabela Island raged from February to July. In 1998–99 the Smithsonian and Imax Ltd. led expeditions to the islands to make their film *Galápagos in 3D*. Below is a journal entry that Smithsonian marine biologist Dr. Carole Baldwin made during the 1999 trip, noting the after-effects of the 1997–98 El Niño.

February 10, 1999, Puerto Ayora

A lot has changed in the six months that we've been away. After the heavy rains of El Niño, it is now about as dry as it gets. Local naturalist Godfrey Merlin told me yesterday at CDRS that this dry spell following El Niño happened in the severe 1983 episode as well. One extreme to the other—truly a tough set of circumstances for the animals and plants. So now, the finches are not nesting, the vegetation is dying (although the Acacia trees are simply brilliant with their masses of orange or yellow flowers), upwelling has apparently resumed leading to large growths of algae (we shall soon see for ourselves), and the marine iguanas are looking nice and fat!

Got a good picture yesterday of a marine iguana on the rocks outside my hotel room. I had just read that one species of finch acts as a "cleaner" of marine iguanas. During cleaning, the iguana apparently stands on all fours like a cat. When I got close enough to the iguana outside my room to get a full-frame shot, there was a finch hopping around on him and picking up things, presumably parasites. This lifestyle of "cleaners" has evolved many times, it seems, at least in birds and fishes. While it's fairly easy to understand how such a relationship between a finch and a vegetarian iguana formed, it's much more difficult to conceptualize the events that led to, for example, a small fish being able to swim safely inside and "clean" the mouth of a large, fish-eating fish!

SELECTED EVENTS IN HISTORY

Note: Most of the events in this chart deal with Ecuadorian and world history. Although the islands are part of Ecuador, historically they were referred to by both English and Spanish names; to avoid confusion we are using only their current Spanish names.

1535
Records attribute the official discovery of the islands to the Bishop of Panama, Fray Tomás de Berlanga, whose ship was becalmed by ocean currents and carried westward while on a journey from Panama to Peru. Bishop Berlanga described the giant tortoises, the iguanas, and the exceptionally tame birds.

1570
Abraham Ortelius draws the first map known to include the Galápagos Islands. The islands were labeled *Insulae de los Galopegos*—Islands of the Tortoises. Navigators of ocean ships often called them *Islas Encantadas* (Enchanted Islands) because of the strong, variable winds and ocean currents that made navigation through them difficult.

1600–1720
Renegades and buccaneers (pirates) use the Galápagos as bases for raids on Spanish colonial ports in South and Central America. The islands supplied them with tortoise meat, fresh water in the rainy season, salt, and limited supplies of firewood.

1790
Alessandro Malaspina of Sicily, employed by the King of Spain, leads the first scientific mission to the Galápagos. Records from this expedition have been lost.

1793
The English captain James Colnett investigates the possibilities for whaling in the island waters and prepares the first reasonably accurate navigational charts of the Galápagos. At about the same time, the first post office barrel is erected on Santa María. Homebound whaling and fishing vessels pick up the mail and deliver it to ports nearer England and the United States.

1795–1895
More than a century of heavy exploitation endangers many Galápagos species. Whalers and sealers capture tortoises for fresh meat. One account says the whalers and sealers removed at least 15,000 tortoises from the islands between 1811 and 1844; another source estimates 100,000. Some species of tortoises were eliminated.

1807–1809
Irishman Patrick Watkins is thought to be the first human to remain in the islands for any length of time. Reports state that he was marooned on Santa María, where he grew vegetables and traded them for rum from visiting whalers.

1813
David Porter, captain of the U.S. warship *Essex*, visits the Galápagos. He succeeds in his mission to destroy the British whaling fleet based in the islands. He also introduces goats to San Salvador Island.

ACTIVITY 3: REPORTS FROM THE GALÁPAGOS

SELECTED EVENTS IN HISTORY

1819
Colombia declares its independence from Spain and claims the provinces of Panama and Ecuador.

1825
Major eruption of Fernandina volcano.

1830
Ecuador secedes from the Great Republic of Colombia and becomes an independent republic.

1832
Ecuador officially annexes the Galápagos and names them *Archipélago del Ecuador*. The Ecuadorian government establishes a penal colony on Floreana.

1835
Charles Darwin visits the islands and sets the stage for a century and a half of scientific investigations.

1836–1940
Settlers make repeated attempts to colonize the islands; most fail. Various island natural resources are exploited—fisheries, tortoises, dyer's moss (a lichen), and salt deposits.

1850–1860
Britain and the United States make several attempts to lease or purchase the Galápagos, but the government of Ecuador resists.

Darwin's *On the Origin of Species* published in 1859.

1861–1865
United States Civil War.

1892
The Government of Ecuador officially designates the islands as *Archipélago de Colón* (Archipelago of Columbus) in honor of the 400th anniversary of Christopher Columbus's (Cristóbal Colón's) first voyage to the Americas. *The Galápagos* remains the most used name.

1898
Spanish-American War.

1914–1918
World War I.

1934
Ecuador enacts the first protective legislation for the environment of the Galápagos.

1941–1945
World War II—United States constructs an air base on the Galápagos Island of Baltra. Land iguanas are eliminated on Baltra.

SELECTED EVENTS IN HISTORY

1955
The International Union for the Conservation of Nature organizes a fact-finding mission to the Galápagos.

1957
The United Nations Educational, Scientific, and Cultural Organization (UNESCO), in cooperation with the International Council for Bird Preservation, the New York Zoological Society, Time Incorporated, and the Government of Ecuador, sends an expedition to the islands to study the state of conservation and to choose a site for a research station.

1959
In honor of the 100th anniversary of the publication of Darwin's *On the Origin of Species*, the Ecuadorian government declares all the islands, except for the areas already settled by colonists, a national park. The Charles Darwin Foundation for the Galápagos Islands is founded to ensure the conservation of unique Galápagos ecosystems and promote the necessary scientific studies.

1968
The National Park Service, under the administration of the Ecuadorian Forestry Service and the Ministry of Agriculture and Livestock, begins to carry out numerous conservation programs.

Fernandina erupts and its caldera collapses.

1969
Organized tourism begins in the Galápagos.

1979
Member states of UNESCO declare the Galápagos Islands a World Heritage Site. This designation recognizes the Galápagos as one of the world's most significant natural areas and part of every human's natural heritage.

1982–1983
El Niño events cause major changes in population of Galápagan plants and animals.

1985
A fire set by humans burns more than 200 sq km of southern Isabela Island.

1986
The Ecuadorian government issues a decree establishing the Galápagos Marine Resources Reserve, embracing 80,000 sq km and extending 15 nautical miles beyond the outer limits of the islands.

1997–1998
A major El Niño event encompasses the Galápagos Islands.

ACTIVITY 4

HOT SPOT VOLCANOES AND ISLAND FORMATION

TEACHER SECTION
This activity is modified from a version created by NSTA for the Smithsonian Institution for the film *Galápagos in 3D*.

Background Information

Teaching about the Galápagos Islands presents a splendid opportunity to study Earth systems science. The geology, geography, climatology, and biology are closely linked in a complex ecological system.

The Galápagos Islands are riding on the Nazca lithospheric plate, which is moving in an east-southeast direction relative to other nearby plates. Just to the north of the Galápagos Archipelago is the Galápagos Spreading Center, a mid-ocean ridge that marks the Nazca and Cocos plate boundaries.

Deep within the Earth at the boundary of the mantle and outer core, mantle material is heated. Because of the tremendous pressure the mantle material does not melt but forms a plume of heat that migrates upward. As the plume gets closer to the surface and pressure is reduced, the mantle material begins to melt and becomes magma (molten rock within the Earth). When the magma nears the boundary of the mantle and lithosphere it collects into large molten pools called magma chambers. The magma makes its way through the crust in a process that involves fracturing, pushing, and melting the overlying rock to erupt at the surface. Magma that erupts onto the surface is called lava. Successive eruptions over long time periods produce the landforms we call volcanoes.

The Galápagos Islands have formed as a result of the Nazca plate moving over a plume of hot material. However, the Galápagos hot spot has not produced the simple linear chain of volcanoes as is seen in the Hawaiian or Society Islands in the Pacific Ocean. Interactions with the nearby Cocos and Pacific plates have somewhat disturbed the orderly island chain development seen elsewhere in the Pacific. Over several million years the Nazca plate has moved slowly east-southeast, with new volcanoes forming over the stationary hot spot now located to the west-northwest of the last eruptive center.

Objective

- To learn how the Galápagos Island chain formed.
- To understand how models help to explain real phenomena, but are not the actual phenomena.
- To understand the concept of plate tectonics and volcanic island formation.

Materials

- Student handouts:
    Hot Spot Volcanoes
    Galápagos Islands and Ages
- Clear plastic box about the size of a shoe box (or glass aquarium)
- Small dropping bottle with a small opening
- Hot and cold tap water
- Red food coloring
- Thin foam panels (similar to white meat-packing trays)
- Marking pen or pencil

ACTIVITY 4: HOT SPOT VOLCANOES AND ISLAND FORMATION

TEACHER SECTION

In addition to studying Earth systems science, this activity presents an opportunity to discuss with students the limitations of laboratory models as opposed to the real world. Scientists use models because they do not have access to the real system in scales of time, space, and materials. Students should realize the limitations of their model. Temperatures within the Earth exceed 2,400 °C, and lava erupts at the surface around 1,200 °C. Mantle material is neither liquid nor solid but somewhere in between. Silicone putty or clay are better analogies for mantle rocks, as they look and feel like a solid but flow under pressure and are brittle when subjected to rapid stress such as a hammer blow.

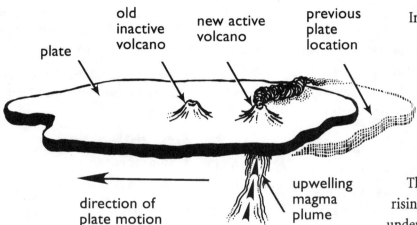

plate

old inactive volcano

new active volcano

previous plate location

direction of plate motion

upwelling magma plume

In this activity, the cold water in the box represents the surrounding material that is cooler than the melted mantle material, represented by the colored water in the dropping bottle. The water in the box represents the Earth's mantle, and the foam plate represents a piece of the Earth's crust. The colored water represents the plume rising through the mantle, staining the underside of the crust. Invite students to compare and contrast their model with the real world. Students should realize that the crust is like a jigsaw puzzle in that the boundaries between plates are narrow zones and not gaps. They should also realize that the mantle material is much more dense than water and that the plate movement is an ongoing slow process—a few centimeters per year—instead of the start and stop process they modeled. If time allows, have the students experiment with ways of improving their model such as thickening the water with gelatin or cornstarch. Be sure students understand they should not change more than one parameter of their model at a time.

This activity not only relates the volcanic origin of the Galápagos Island chain, but also can illustrate the important ecological concept of what needs to happen to a newly formed environment before colonizing plants and animals can take hold and survive. The formation of volcanic islands is a perfect springboard into a discussion of volcanism, rock weathering, and soil formation and how the forces that shape the Earth are integral to our understanding of island biogeography.

ACTIVITY 4: HOT SPOT VOLCANOES AND ISLAND FORMATION

As an extension, have the students in each group investigate each of the islands from the student handout *Age of Galápagos Islands and Eruptive Cycles*. They could describe the general geology of each island, including the level of soil formation (mostly lava, some lava/some soil, mostly soil/some lava, etc.). Students could also describe the amount of plant colonization and plant habitat formation on each island, as the newer islands (those with the most recent eruptions and thus formed most recently) will have the greatest amount of fresh lava flows and the least amount of soil formation; those that are older will have more soil and greater plant diversity.

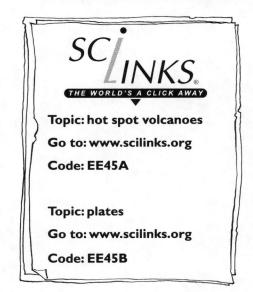

SCI LINKS
THE WORLD'S A CLICK AWAY

Topic: hot spot volcanoes
Go to: www.scilinks.org
Code: EE45A

Topic: plates
Go to: www.scilinks.org
Code: EE45B

Procedure

Divide your students into teams of three or four and distribute the materials listed above. Once students have completed the hot spot activity, discuss the limitations of laboratory models as opposed to the real world. The activity will take approximately 30 minutes. Allow about 20 minutes for discussion, and allocate additional time for students to read further about hot spots, volcanoes, and the geology of the Galápagos Islands.

Answers to student questions:

1. Describe what happened when you submerged the small bottle in the water.

When the small bottle is placed in the box the colored water in the box will flow out in a stream toward the surface.

2. Explain why you think it happened.

The warm, colored water in the bottle is less dense than the cold water in the box. Thus, it rises through the cooler water in response to gravity. The cold water flows into the bottle, displacing the hot water as it flows out.

plate

active volcano

volcano chain

3. Sketch an outline of your lithospheric plate and show the locations of the plume stains. If the stains on your plate model represent volcanoes, place a small circle where you think the next volcano would erupt.

Sketches will vary but should show a chain of stain marks from the starting point with a circle at the end.

ACTIVITY 4: HOT SPOT VOLCANOES AND ISLAND FORMATION

TEACHER SECTION

4. How is your model like the Earth's interior?
Explanations will vary but students should understand that the small bottle of hot colored water represents hot core material that becomes less dense as it moves through the relatively cooler mantle material, represented by the cold tap water in the box.

5. What are some of the limitations of your model compared to the actual causes of volcanic eruptions?
Limitations to the model include temperature, pressure, currents, viscosity of both the plume and the surrounding mantle, scale, and time.

6. Study the table that lists the ages of the Galápagos Islands. What does that tell you about the relative movement of the Nazca plate?
The age of eruptions are relatively older toward the east-southeast. This implies that the Nazca plate is moving in that direction. This simplistic answer is actually more complicated because the Galápagos Islands are near the juncture of three moving plates.

7. Which of the Galápagos Islands would you predict to have active volcanoes? Which would you predict to have extinct volcanoes? Explain.
The currently active volcanoes are located on the western end of the Galápagos Archipelago.

8. Where and why do you think the next Galápagos Island will form? Why do you think this?
If the movement continues towards the east-southeast, the next group of islands should form to the northwest or west of the existing island group.

Standards

The material promoted in this activity enhances and supports student understanding of the following *National Science Education Standards* for grades 5–8:

Structure of the Earth System (Earth and Space Science)

The solid Earth is layered with a lithosphere; hot, convecting mantle; and dense, metallic core.

Lithospheric plates on the scales of continents and oceans constantly move at rates of centimeters per year in response to movements in the mantle. Major geological events, such as earthquakes, volcanic eruptions, and mountain building, result from these plate motions.

Land forms are the result of a combination of constructive and destructive forces. Constructive forces include crystal deformation, volcanic eruption, and deposition of sediment, while destructive forces include weathering and erosion.

Some changes in the solid Earth can be described as the *rock cycle*. Old rocks at the Earth's surface weather, forming sediments that are buried, then compacted, heated, and often recrystallized into new rock. Eventually, those new rocks may be brought to the surface by the forces that drive plate motions, and the rock cycle continues.

Soil consists of weathered rocks and decomposed organic material from dead plants, animals, and bacteria. Soils are often found in layers, with each having a different chemical composition and texture.

Earth's History (Earth and Space Science)

The Earth processes we see today, including erosion, movement of lithospheric plates, and changes in atmospheric composition, are similar to those that occurred in the past. Earth history is also influenced by occasional catastrophes, such as the impact of an asteroid or comet.

Assessment

Activity	Exemplary	Emergent	Deficient
Part A	Students are able to follow all laboratory instructions and to create a workable model of volcanic hot spots with little teacher direction. Students can answer all student questions and accurately predict where the next island(s) will form.	Students are able to set up the volcanic model but need teacher direction to make it work. Students can answer some questions but do not understand how to predict where the next island(s) will form.	Students have great difficulty setting up the model by themselves. Teacher help is necessary for them to do the lab. They do not easily answer the student questions and cannot relate their results to what formed the Galápagos Islands.

HOT SPOT VOLCANOES

Far from being random occurrences, volcanoes are a result of physical events taking place both deep in the Earth's interior and at its surface. Earth's surface is a thin, rigid, relatively cool crust (the *lithosphere*) that is broken into a number of pieces or, as geologists call them, *plates*. These plates are in motion relative to one another. Many of the volcanoes with which we are familiar, such as Mount St. Helens or Mount Vesuvius, occur at or near the boundaries of these lithospheric plates.

However, some volcanoes form within the boundaries of the lithosphere as the plate passes over a plume of hot material rising through the mantle. Geologists call these "hot spot" volcanoes. In time, as a plate continues moving over a hot spot, the old volcano becomes extinct, and a new volcano forms. The Hawaiian Islands are an example of this type of activity. The Galápagos Islands, riding on the Nazca plate, are over a hot spot, but do not form a simple chain like the Hawaiian Islands. Study the handout *Galápagos Islands and Ages* to see if you can detect a pattern in the volcanic eruptions.

Procedure

Read all of the instructions and questions prior to beginning the activity. Select a team member to record your observations and answers.

1. Collect the materials for this activity from your teacher.

2. Fill the plastic box with enough cold tap water to cover the small bottle by several centimeters.

3. Prepare your lithospheric plate model by cutting the foam to fit about 1/3 of the box length. Mark one end of the plate with an "S" so you will know your starting point.

4. Place 5–10 drops of food coloring in the small bottle and fill it to the top with hot tap water.

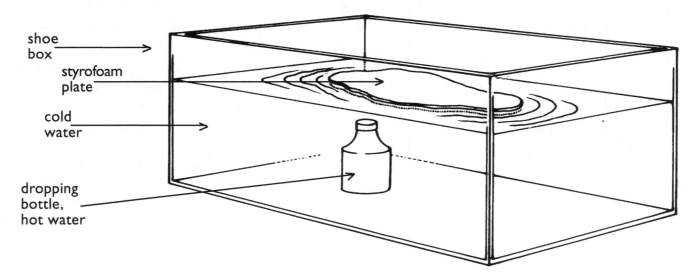

ACTIVITY 4: HOT SPOT VOLCANOES AND ISLAND FORMATION

HOT SPOT VOLCANOES

5. Carefully place the bottle in the center of the box without tilting it. Watch the colored water and write your initial observations.

6. Gently place your model plate on the water so that one end is over the bottle. Hold it steady. After the colored plume has risen enough to stain the underside of the model, move your model about two centimeters and hold it still again. Repeat until there is no more room on the model plate.

Answer the following questions:

1. Describe what happened when you submerged the small bottle in the water.

2. Explain why you think it happened.

3. Sketch an outline of your lithospheric plate and show the locations of the plume stains. If the stains on your plate model represent volcanoes, place a small circle where you think the next volcano would erupt.

4. How is your model like the Earth's interior?

HOT SPOT VOLCANOES

5. What are some of the limitations of your model compared to the actual causes for volcanic eruptions?

6. Study the table that lists the ages of the Galápagos Islands. What does that tell you about the relative movement of the Nazca plate?

7. Which of the Galápagos Islands would you predict to have active volcanoes? Which would you predict to have extinct volcanoes? Explain.

8. Where and why do you think the next Galápagos Island will form? Why do you think this?

ACTIVITY 4: HOT SPOT VOLCANOES AND ISLAND FORMATION

GALÁPAGOS ISLANDS AND AGES

Age of Galápagos Islands and Eruptive Cycles	
Fernandina	Historic and ongoing eruptions
Isabela	Historic and ongoing eruptions
Darwin	Less than 10,000 years ago
San Salvador	Less than 10,000 years ago
Genovesa	Less than 10,000 years ago
Marchena	Less than 10,000 years ago
Pinzón	1,000,000 years ago
Santa Cruz	More than 1,000,000 years ago
San Cristóbal	More than 2,500,000 years ago
Santa Fé	Extinct
Española	Extinct

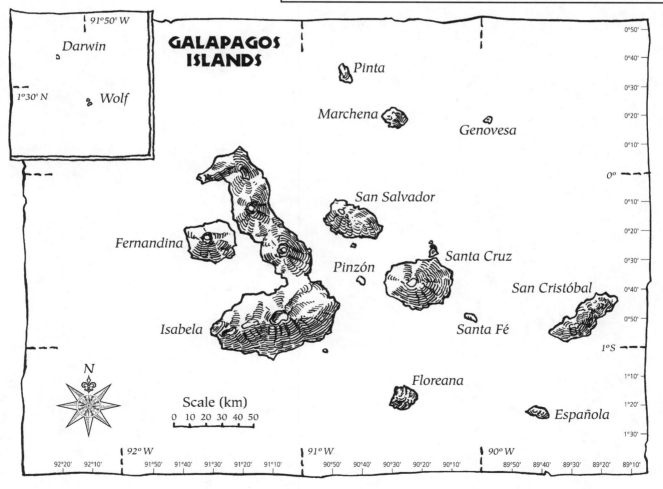

ECOLOGY AND ISLANDS

CHAPTER 2

CURRENT EVENTS IN THE OCEAN

TEACHER SECTION
This activity is modified from a version created by NSTA for the Smithsonian Institution for the film *Galápagos in 3D*.

Background Information

Islands by definition are isolated by a body of water. Despite this isolation, life arrives; because of the isolation, it often thrives. Sometimes, an island originates from part of a larger land mass, and when separated, the flora and fauna go with it. However, in the case of island chains formed from hot spot volcanoes, they are completely devoid of life when the molten lava hardens above the surface into a viable land mass. Plant and animal life arrive at isolated volcanic islands, such as the Galápagos, in a number of ways, with water and air currents playing a crucial role. Later activities explore this in greater depth.

Currents, large-scale movements of water, occur throughout the surface and subsurface layers of the ocean. Wind moving over water drags surface water along its path, creating surface currents. This activity allows students to simulate the flow of major ocean currents and experiment with how land formations and variations in wind direction can affect ocean currents. It is important, however, to lead students to the understanding that many factors determine current formation in the ocean and that this model presents just one of them. Current formation is a complex aspect of oceanography.

The prevailing winds in the Pacific are called the *trade winds*. (As an extra activity, you may want to have your students investigate how these winds became known as the trade winds.) The trade winds that move air over the South Pacific from the southeast toward the northwest are called *South Easterlies*. Near the Galápagos, these winds move up along the coast of Peru and then out towards the Galápagos. This wind pattern moves the ocean waters in the same direction, forming the *Humboldt Current*.

In the eastern Pacific, as the surface water current moves along the South American coast, off-shore winds push it westward allowing cooler, deeper water to come to the surface and to the Galápagos Islands. In addition, the South Equatorial Current moves warm water from the Panama Current directly from the coast of Ecuador west to the Galápagos.

Objective

- To investigate how landforms and wind affect ocean surface currents. These concepts relate to the ways in which life arrives to islands.

Materials

- World map

For each team:

- Student handouts:

    Current Events in the Ocean

    Surface Currents of the Pacific

    Currents Near the Galápagos

- Clear plastic shoebox or metal baking pan (a translucent box will allow students to use the handouts to trace the continents)
- Non-permanent marker
- Plasticine (non-water soluble) modeling clay
- Black permanent marker
- Dark food coloring
- Paper towels

For each student:

- Plastic drinking straw with a flexible elbow

TEACHER SECTION

Sci LINKS.
THE WORLD'S A CLICK AWAY

Topic: wind currents

Go to: www.scilinks.org

Code: EE56

This movement of surface water away from the coast, which brings cold subsurface waters to the surface, is a process known as *upwelling*. This cold, nutrient-rich, upwelled water supports an abundance of sea life along the coast of South America and the Galápagos Islands. Biologists have discovered that many marine species are unusually dense in the Galápagos waters. They theorize that this is because of the nutrient-enriched water that first provides food to enormous numbers of microscopic life forms. These life forms then become food for small crustaceans and fish, which in turn become food for larger organisms. Because the increased nutrients in the water bolster the entire food chain, the area can support more life of all sizes.

In the Galápagos, therefore, some predator species, such as hammerhead sharks or barracudas, appear in large schools—a behavior that is seldom seen anywhere else in the world. Thus the movements of water, both because of ocean currents and ocean upwellings, help determine which organisms reach newly formed islands to colonize them.

Procedure

Using a map of the world, point out the flow of ocean waters in the Humboldt Current (along the coast of South America). Then divide students into groups of two or four and distribute the student handout *Current Events in the Ocean*. Monitor the students as they follow the directions.

Standards

The material promoted in this activity enhances and supports student understanding of the following *National Science Education Standards* for grades 5–8:

Understandings About Scientific Inquiry (Science as Inquiry)

Different kinds of questions suggest different kinds of scientific investigations. Some investigations involve observing and describing objects, organisms, or events; some involve collecting specimens; some involve experiments; some involve seeking more information; some involve discovery of new objects and phenomena; and some involve making models.

Structure of the Earth System (Earth and Space Science)   **TEACHER SECTION**

Global patterns of atmospheric movement influence local weather.
Oceans have a major effect on climate because water in the oceans holds
a large amount of heat.

Assessment

Activity	Exemplary	Emergent	Deficient
	Students are able to set up the laboratory model with little help from the teacher. They easily follow all directions and successfully demonstrate how ocean currents influence landforms and how landforms influence ocean currents. They describe the relationship between wind and ocean currents and how variables such as wind direction, wind speed, land formations, etc., seem to be related to ocean current patterns.	Students are able to set up the laboratory model but have some difficulty actually running the lab. They are able to see how ocean currents work but have difficulty working with or describing how other variables such as wind direction, wind speed, land formations, etc., seem to be related to ocean current patterns.	Students are not able to set up the laboratory model without teacher help. They cannot get their laboratory model to work correctly. Students are not able to see relationships between ocean currents, wind patterns, landforms, etc.

CURRENT EVENTS IN THE OCEAN

Sailors have known for centuries that ocean currents—large-scale movements of water—can speed up or slow down a ship, just as airplane pilots know that it takes longer to fly from New York to California than the reverse because of the jet stream. In modern times, scientists have discovered that ocean currents have major effects on weather patterns and on the ecology of the ocean and nearby land masses. One type of current is called a surface current, which, as you might have guessed, flows across the surface of the ocean almost like a river flows across dry land. However, a surface current lacks the solid banks of a river to direct its flow. As a result, the direction of a surface current may change when the wind blowing across it shifts, when it encounters warmer or colder water, or when it nears land. This activity will show how surface currents are affected by the direction of the wind.

Procedure

1. Using the handout *Currents Near the Galápagos* as a guide, draw an outline of the western coast of North and South America near the right side of the pan or plastic shoebox with a crayon or non-permanent marker.

2. Following the outline pattern, place ridges of modeling clay about 3–5 cm high along the bottom of the pan to contain the "ocean." Press the clay firmly to the pan or plastic box and smooth the gaps between the clay and the pan. It is important to create a watertight seal to prevent "oceanic" leaks, and have your clay be high enough to contain the water.

3. Create some island masses out of clay, about 3 cm west of South America at the position of the equator. This will represent the Galápagos Islands.

4. Fill the ocean area of your model with water. Pour slowly, without overflowing the ridge. Wait for the water to settle.

5. Bend the straw at the elbow. Write your name on the short end of the straw with the permanent marker. This will identify your straw and remind you which end of the straw to point toward the water. Do not put the short end of the straw with your name on it into your mouth.

CURRENT EVENTS IN THE OCEAN

6. Try not to touch the pan or plastic box as you take turns doing the following:

- Hold your straw upside-down above the water, so that the short end (the end you usually blow through) is parallel to the ocean surface.

- Point your straw from the lower tip of South America toward the equator.

- Have your partner place one or two drops of food coloring in the water near the short end of your straw.

- As soon as the food coloring is in the water blow gently through the straw and observe the patterns of ocean currents produced by wind.

7. Repeat step 6 a few more times to develop a sense of the relationship between wind direction, landmass configuration, and current patterns. You may need to get clean water if the "ocean" becomes too dark from food coloring.

8. Repeat step 6 once more, but this time blow gently along the coast of Central America towards South America (from north to south). This action represents the Panama Current that brings warmer water to the northern Galápagos Islands.

9. Clean up your workstation, using the paper towels to wipe up any spilled water.

10. Describe the relationship between wind and ocean currents. How do variables such as wind direction, wind speed, land formations, etc., seem to be related to ocean current patterns?

SURFACE CURRENTS OF THE PACIFIC

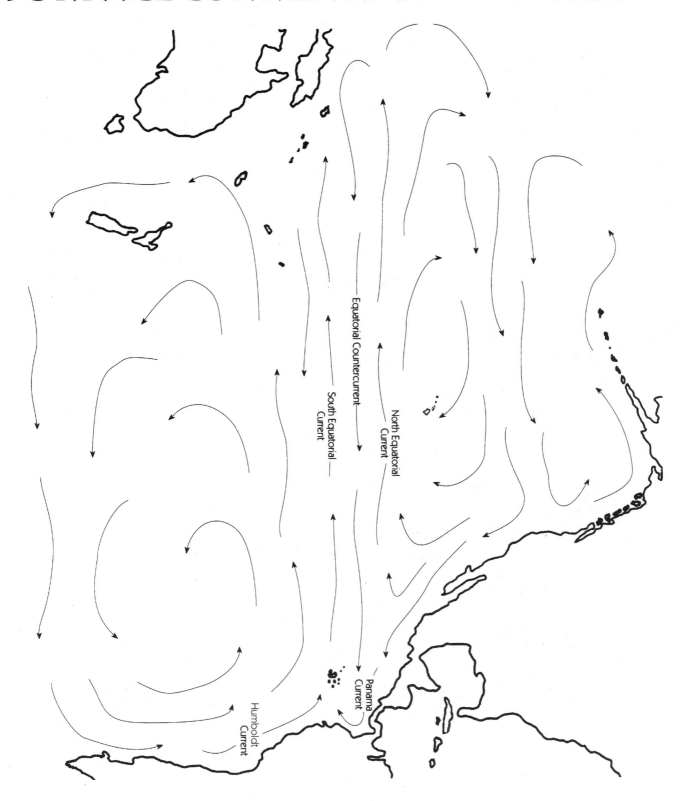

CURRENTS NEAR THE GALÁPAGOS

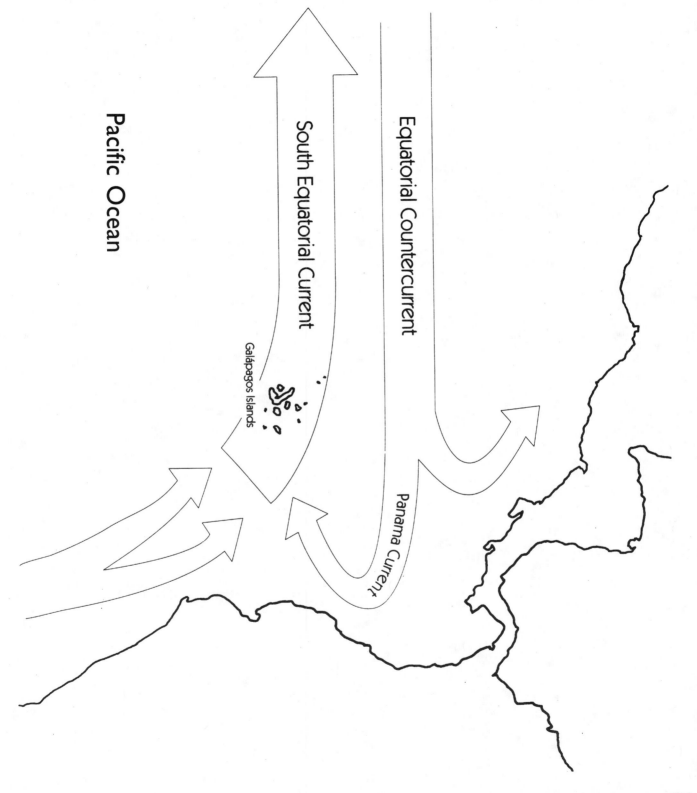

Pacific Ocean

South Equatorial Current

Equatorial Countercurrent

Galápagos Islands

Panama Current

HOT SIDE HOT, COOL SIDE COOL

TEACHER SECTION

This activity is modified from a version created by NSTA for the Smithsonian Institution for the film *Galapagos in 3D*.

Background Information

This activity will help students visualize what happens when liquids of different densities meet. Warm water is less dense than cold and the two will not readily mix. As the cold Humboldt Current flows up the South American coast it tends to keep the warm Panama Current from reaching the Galápagos.

As was demonstrated in the previous activity, *Current Events in the Ocean*, the cold water of the Humboldt Current flows north along the South American coast until the current is forced west towards the Galápagos Islands. This cold dense water is filled with nutrients. As the cold water reaches the shallow regions of the Galápagos Islands it is forced up to the top (upwelled), bringing its nutrients to the surface and to the marine organisms that dwell in the shallow waters. The richness of the upwelled water provides an abundance of nutrients for these organisms. The food web that results from this nutrient abundance extends from the ocean waters out to the island ecosystems themselves. Eventually, the warm (less dense) water pushes over the colder (more dense) water, still not mixing with it. When this happens, the warm water reaches the northern islands and brings warm water species with it.

This phenomenon is a good springboard for a discussion about how geology, oceanography, and ecology are interrelated—the shape of the landforms impacts the flow of water, which influences the habitats and ecosystems of the entire island chain.

This activity demonstrates how currents form as cold and warm water meet, how cold water sinks when released into warm water, and how warm water rises when released into cold.

Objectives

- To understand how cold and warm ocean currents interact, and the effect they have on nearby land masses.

Materials

For each team:

- Student handout:

    Hot Side Hot, Cool Side Cool

- Clear plastic shoebox or small aquarium

- 250 ml beaker

- Two small plastic drinking cups

- Water

- Food coloring

- Two thumb tacks or push pins

- Weights or small stones

- Ice

- Paper

- Pencils

ACTIVITY 6: HOT SIDE HOT, COOL SIDE COOL

TEACHER SECTION

SCiLINKS
THE WORLD'S A CLICK AWAY

Topic: ocean currents

Go to: www.scilinks.org

Code: EE64

Procedure

Divide the class into partners, and distribute the materials. Supervise the students as they set up their workstations. Use the illustrations on the student handout *Hot Side Hot, Cool Side Cool* for guidance.

Another option is to divide your class into teams and provide each with the materials, instead of handing out the worksheet directions. Have the students devise their own methods for observing the effects when warm and cool currents meet. Each team can prepare a report of its procedure and findings to the rest of the class.

As an extension, once students have explored this model of cold and warm mixing, ask them to suggest modifications that would improve their model to make it more closely resemble the Galápagos currents. To accomplish this, they may need to do more research to come up with the information we have provided in the teacher section.

Standards

The material promoted in this activity enhances and supports student understanding of the following *National Science Education Standards* for grades 5–8:

Transfer of Energy (Physical Science)

Energy is a property of many substances and is associated with heat, light, electricity, mechanical motion, sound, nuclei, and the nature of a chemical. Energy is transferred in many ways.

Heat moves in predictable ways, flowing from warmer objects to cooler ones, until both reach the same temperature.

Populations and Ecosystems (Life Science)

Populations of organisms can be categorized by the function they serve in an ecosystem. Plants and some microorganisms are producers—they make their own food. All animals, including humans, are consumers, which obtain food by eating other organisms. Decomposers, primarily bacteria and fungi, are consumers that use waste materials and dead organisms for food. Food webs identify the relationships among producers, consumers, and decomposers in an ecosystem.

The number of organisms an ecosystem can support depends on the resources available and abiotic factors, such as quantity of light and water, range of temperatures, and soil composition. Given adequate biotic and abiotic resources and no disease or predators, populations (including humans) increase at rapid rates. Lack of resources and other factors, such as predation and climate, limit the growth of populations in specific niches in the ecosystem.

TEACHER SECTION

Assessment

Activity	Exemplary	Emergent	Deficient
	Students follow the activity instructions closely and are able to show the hot and cold water currents in the laboratory models. The students are able to answer all the questions from the worksheet and relate the model to the real ocean currents. Students can explain the reasons for the differences between the hot and cold variations of the lab.	Students follow the laboratory instructions but the results are not completely clear or not all members of the group experienced or understood the results. Some of the questions are answered, but some are not or are only partly complete. Students have trouble explaining the difference between the hot and cold variations and relating this activity to real-life situations.	Students do not follow the instructions for the lab or do not understand what it means. Students have little knowledge of how this activity relates to real life.

HOT SIDE HOT, COOL SIDE COOL

Considering that these islands are placed directly under the equator, the climate is far from being excessively hot; this seems chiefly caused by the singularly low temperature of the surrounding water, brought here by the great southern Polar current.

Charles Darwin, *Voyage of the Beagle*, 1845

Darwin described the cold waters at the Earth's hottest latitude in 1845. Why do ocean currents bring cold waters to regions that are at the equator? Why don't warm waters mix with these cold water currents? What happens when cold water meets warm water? The climate of an island or coastal region depends upon the movement of cold and warm water in its surrounding oceans. This activity will help you explore what happens when cold and warm water meet.

Most people know that hot air rises—just watch the flight of a hot air balloon or feel the temperature rise as you climb the stairs on a warm summer day. Why does warm air rise above cold? Warm air is less dense than cold air and therefore floats above the heavier cold air in a room. Is this also true with water? Let's investigate. Use the illustrations for guidance.

Hot Side Hot

1. Fill the plastic shoebox or aquarium with cool water and a few ice cubes, making sure you keep the water level below the height of the plastic cup (for example, if your cup is 8 cm tall, make sure the water in the box is only 6.5 cm high). Wait a couple of minutes for the water to cool down.

2. With one of your pins, punch a hole in the side of the plastic cup about 2–3 cm from the bottom. Repeat with the other pin on the other side. Leave the pins in the cup to act as temporary plugs.

3. Fill the cup with warm water and add three or four drops of food coloring. Stir the water to make sure the color is completely mixed.

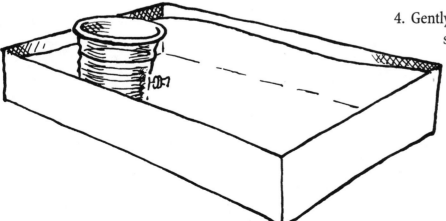

4. Gently place the cup in the water-filled shoebox (the cup may need to be weighted down with stones or weights to stay at the bottom). Put the cup all the way to one side of the container, and wait for the water to become still, but don't wait too long and let the water in the cup cool down.

HOT SIDE HOT, COOL SIDE COOL

5. Quickly and carefully remove the pins. Plan your procedure before you try it. As much as possible, try not to disrupt the water in the container. If no water leaves the cup, you may have to make the pin holes a little larger.

6. Describe what you observed when the warm, colored water entered the cool water in the container. In which direction did the warm water flow?

Cool Side Cool

Repeat the whole process using warm water in the shoebox and cool water and food coloring in the plastic cup.

1. Fill the plastic shoebox or aquarium with lukewarm water, making sure you keep the water level below the height of the plastic cup.

2. Place two ice cubes in a 250 ml beaker, and add cool tap water. Add three or four drops of food coloring to the ice water in the beaker and stir.

3. Wait a couple of minutes for the colored water in the beaker to cool down.

4. With one of your pins, punch a hole in the side of the plastic cup about 2–3 cm from the bottom. Repeat with the other pin on the other side. Leave the pins in the cup; they act as temporary plugs.

5. Fill the cup with the colored ice water well above the level of the pins, and gently place the cup in the water-filled shoebox (the cup may need to be weighted down with stones or weights to stay at the bottom). Put the cup all the way to one side of the container, and wait for the water to become still.

6. Carefully remove the pins. Plan your procedure before you try it. As much as possible, try not to disrupt the water in the container. If no water leaves the cup, you may have to make the pin holes a little larger.

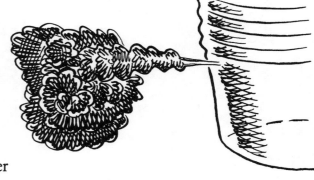

7. Describe what you observed when the cold, colored water entered the warm water in the container. Where did the cold water flow? What happened when the colored water hit the bottom of the container?

Write up the results of your experiments. Based on what you've just observed, explain what might happen when the cold Humboldt Current meets the warm Panama Current near the Galápagos Islands.

CLIMATE DIVERSITY

Background Information

Because some of the Galápagos Islands reach heights of 1,000 m, the climate at the higher elevations is very different from the climate near the shore. Thus on any one island, different *microhabitats* exist because of the dramatically different temperatures and rainfall levels at different elevations. These habitats are referred to as *vegetative zones*.

The vegetative zones on the Galápagos Islands include a Coastal Zone along the ocean's edge, an Arid Zone, a Scalesia Zone, a Miconia Zone, and a Fern Zone in the highlands. Each of these zones has a characteristic pattern of temperature and rainfall. As you venture from the coast and climb in altitude through the Arid Zone up to the Fern Zone, the amount of rainfall increases. The Fern Zone can receive as much as 2.5 m of rainfall in a year. As the climate gets wetter and cooler, the types of plants and animals that thrive are different from those of the drier areas. Each zone is a different community.

This section ties into the earlier activities on currents because, as shown in the *Vegetative Zones of the Galápagos* handout, wind currents as well as elevation will affect how much moisture an area of an island receives. Although rain is infrequent in the Galápagos, the *prevailing winds* of the Humboldt Current bring moist air to the south sides of the islands. As this moisture cools, it results in misty precipitation high on the south sides of the mountains. You may wish to review the *water cycle* with your students before continuing. This activity also connects to later sections on biodiversity and food webs because the different zones affect the types of plants and animals that can live there.

Objectives

- To learn about the different vegetative zones of the Galápagos Islands and how each zone is influenced by weather patterns.

- To learn how scientists use climatograms to identify weather patterns within a specific area.

- To use precipitation and temperature data from the Coastal Zone and Fern Zone to construct climatograms.

- To compare the weather patterns of the two vegetative zones.

- To develop and examine a climatogram of students' own community.

Materials

- Student handouts:

    Climate Diversity on an Island

    Plant Species of the Galápagos

    Vegetative Zones of the Galápagos

    Construct Your Own Climatograms

    Blank Climatograms (optional)

- Graph paper

- Pencils

- Rulers

TEACHER SECTION

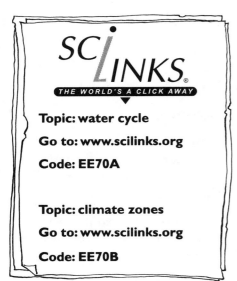

Topic: water cycle

Go to: www.scilinks.org

Code: EE70A

Topic: climate zones

Go to: www.scilinks.org

Code: EE70B

One way that scientists identify these ecological differences is with a *climatogram*, a graph that displays information about a climate. The precipitation is depicted as a bar graph with its scale on the left-hand side; the temperature is depicted as a line graph with its scale on the right-hand side. Explain to the students that precipitation does not necessarily mean rain; it can also mean snow, sleet, or even condensation such as morning dew. The patterns formed by these data for a given zone can be compared to patterns formed by the data for other zones.

In this activity, students will read about and look at some climatograms, and then create climatograms for the Coastal Zone and Fern Zone of Santa Cruz Island. This will also help them understand the extreme range of weather patterns existing on a single island.

Procedure

Separate students into teams of three or four; give each team a copy of the student handout *Vegetative Zones of the Galápagos*. Have them review the diagram and the descriptions of each zone, and ask them to note the weather patterns and vegetation found in each. Explain that the temperature and precipitation of each zone influences what organisms live there.

Next distribute the graph paper and student handout *Climate Diversity* worksheet. As students read this worksheet, review the purpose of a climatogram and discuss how to create one on graph paper. Depending on the skill level of your students, you may wish to distribute the *Blank Climatograms* worksheet rather than have students create their own on graphs.

After completing the sections using Galápagos data, have students create a climatogram for their local community and ask them to draw parallels and make predictions about local vegetation. You can obtain precipitation and temperature data from the newspaper or local cooperative extension agency.

Answers to student questions:

1. Compare your climatogram of the Coastal Zone to that of the Fern Zone. How do precipitation and temperature change from zone to zone? Which weather factor is similar in both zones and which is different?

> The Coastal Zone receives much less moisture than the Fern Zone, because there is less precipitation and because the clouds that hover over the higher Fern Zone provide moisture through condensation. Air

temperature is similar in both zones, and relatively constant, while the amount of precipitation varies a great deal.

2. *Within each zone, which weather factor is more consistent (stays the same)? Which factor fluctuates (changes) throughout the year?*

The temperature does not vary much throughout the year, whereas both zones have a wet season.

3. *The Galápagos Islands usually have two seasons: a wet season and a dry season. Using the climatograms, determine when the wet season begins and how long it lasts.*

The wet season begins in late March or April and lasts through May.

4. *Describe how you think plant and animal life might be affected by the wide variation in the amount of precipitation in the Galápagos. Would you expect plants and animals similar to those of the deserts of the American Southwest or more like Florida, or somewhere else? Explain your answer.*

Most species of plants will tend to be found in only one or two zones because they are adapted for certain levels of moisture, and animals that are adapted to eat those types of plants will be found similarly. Because the zones are so different, students should expect to find a wide variety of plants. Those in the Arid Zone will be more like plants in the American Southwest, whereas those in the Coastal Zone would be more like plants in Florida. Plants in the highlands would be similar to plants found in the Pacific Northwest.

5. *At the summits of the higher islands, water from the clouds that rest on the peaks condenses onto vegetation. How might this make the growing conditions different between the higher and lower elevations on these islands?*

Only plants with a tolerance of higher moisture levels can survive at the higher elevations. Animals adapted to eat those plants will also be found there.

6. *The prevailing wind causes the clouds (and the rain) to come from the south. How might this affect the size of the Arid Zone on the south side of Santa Cruz? On the north side? How might this affect the Miconia or Fern Zones on the south side of the island? On the north side?*

The Arid Zones will be smaller and not extend as high up on the south sides of the islands because the clouds containing moisture will approach from that direction. The north sides of the islands will be the opposite.

TEACHER SECTION

7. What kinds of plants would you expect to find in the Arid Zone? In the Scalesia Zone? In the Miconia Zone? In the Fern Zone?

Arid Zone plants are adapted to go long periods without water (like cactus). The higher up the zone is in elevation, the more the plants in that zone will rely on water.

Below are answer keys to the climatograms

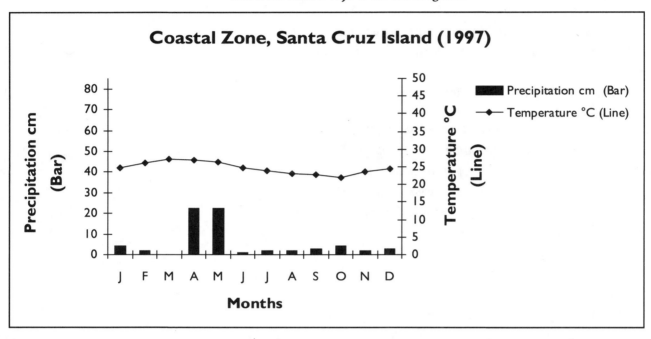

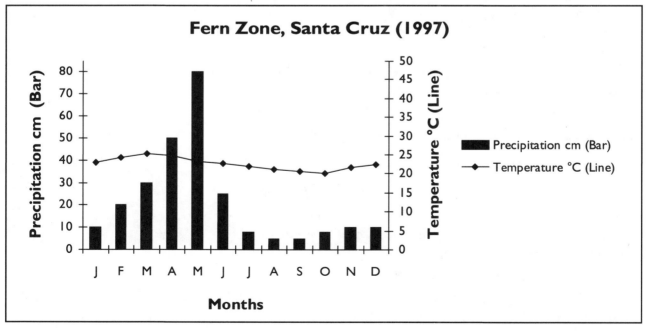

Standards

The material promoted in this activity enhances and supports student understanding of the following *National Science Education Standards* for grades 5–8:

Populations and Ecosystems (Life Science)

A population consists of all individuals of a species that occur together at a given place and time. All populations living together and the physical factors with which they interact compose an ecosystem.

The number of organisms an ecosystem can support depends on the resources available and abiotic factors, such as quantity of light and water, range of temperatures, and soil composition. Given adequate biotic and abiotic resources and no disease or predators, populations (including humans) increase at rapid rates. Lack of resources and other factors, such as predation and climate, limit the growth of populations in specific niches in the ecosystem.

Structure of the Earth System (Earth and Space Science)

Land forms are the result of a combination of constructive and destructive forces. Constructive forces include crustal deformation, volcanic eruption, and deposition of sediment, while destructive forces include weathering and erosion.

Water, which covers the majority of Earth's surface, circulates through the crust, oceans, and atmosphere in what is known as the "water cycle." Water evaporates from Earth's surface, rises and cools as it moves to higher elevations, condenses as rain or snow, and falls to the surface where it collects in lakes, oceans, soil, and in rocks underground.

Clouds, formed by the condensation of water vapor, affect weather and climate.

TEACHER SECTION

Assessment

Activity	Exemplary	Emergent	Deficient
Part A	Students are able to construct climatograms from the data provided. They can answer all the analysis questions correctly by interpreting the climatograms they have constructed.	Students are able to construct climatograms from the provided data with some help from other students or from the teacher. They can answer only some questions by interpreting their graphs.	Students have difficulty constructing climatograms from the provided data. They can answer few questions about the climate of the Galápagos Islands.
Extension	Students are able to get local climate data and construct a climatogram from this data.	Students have trouble getting local data but can graph it if provided.	Students cannot get data and have trouble graphing data if provided.

CLIMATE DIVERSITY ON AN ISLAND

When visiting a new study site, a naturalist always notes the weather patterns. These patterns largely determine which plants and animals can live there. A *limiting factor* is an element of the environment that is important in determining what organisms can survive. This activity looks at moisture as a limiting factor in the Galápagos Islands. The amount of moisture available to organisms depends on both precipitation patterns (rain, sleet, or snow, for example) and temperature. How the zones appear on the islands may be the result of both elevation and *prevailing winds,* which may bring more moisture to one side of an island over another.

Climatograms

The average weather data of an area can be graphed to allow scientists to identify patterns. One way to do this is with a *climatogram,* a graph that clearly displays information about a climate. The precipitation is shown as a bar graph with its scale on the left-hand side; the temperature is shown as a line graph with its scale on the right-hand side. The patterns formed by these data can be compared to patterns on climatograms of other zones or biomes.

The Galápagos Islands usually have two seasons: a *wet season* and a *dry season.* In most years, the wet season begins in December and lasts for about five months. However, sometimes there are years when there is more than usual or less than usual amounts of rainfall. For example, in 1977 there was virtually no precipitation in the islands at all. Very wet years occur every two to seven years, caused by an ocean and weather pattern known as El Niño. In 1997–98, the Galápagos experienced one of the strongest El Niño events in recorded history. Rain fell almost non-stop, and by the end of the year, more than four times the record annual precipitation had fallen.

The following climatogram shows the variations of the wet and dry season for the Coastal Zone of San Cristóbal, located approximately 75 km southeast of Santa Cruz. The temperature remains fairly constant as the seasons change. The island of Santa Cruz also exhibits another interesting climatic pattern—vegetative zones. This activity will explore the various climatic zones found on Santa Cruz Island.

Because of their volcanic origins, some of the islands reach heights of 1,000 m, and the climate at the higher elevations is much different than it is near the shore. Many *microhabitats* exist on the islands because dramatically different temperatures and rainfall levels occur at different elevations. These habitats are referred to as *vegetative zones.*

The vegetative zones on the Galápagos Islands include a Coastal Zone along the ocean's edge, an Arid Zone, a Scalesia Zone, a Miconia Zone, and a Fern Zone in the highlands. Each of these zones has a characteristic pattern of temperature and rainfall. As you venture from the coast and climb in altitude through the Arid Zone up to the Fern Zone, the amount of rainfall increases. The Fern Zone can receive as much as 2.5 m of rainfall in a year. Of course, as the climate gets wetter and cooler, the types of plants and animals that thrive are different from those in the drier areas. Each zone is a different community.

PLANT SPECIES OF THE GALÁPAGOS

Coastal Zone: Salt Resistant Plants

Mangrove—Several species of flowering mangrove shrubs and trees grow at water's edge. Their branches may reach as high as 25 m. Most mangroves are able to resist salt (filter the salt water so its leaves receive fresh water), conserve water, and absorb oxygen from the air. Their roots are shallow but spread out over a wide distance. Mangroves send out prop roots from their branches to help anchor the plant. The tangle of their roots gives shelter to many small fish and marine animals.

Arid Zone: Dry Area Plants

Prickly Pear Cactus—This cactus grows up to 12 m with a thick trunk, flat pads, spines, yellow flowers, and greenish fruit.

Candelabra Cactus—This species grows to about 7 m high. Its branches look like organ pipes or like the arms of a giant candelabra.

Lava Cactus—This is a short, thick cactus only about 12 cm high. Each branch is covered with many spines and lasts only a few years. Its flowers open before dawn and shrivel by 7 or 8 a.m.

Galápagos Tomato—This variety of tomato is a small plant with spear-shaped leaves and small yellow or red fruit. Its seeds have evolved a thick coat to resist salt and drying. They usually sprout only after passing through the intestines of a tortoise or a mockingbird.

PLANT SPECIES OF THE GALÁPAGOS

Scalesia, Miconia, and Fern Zones: Humid Area Plants

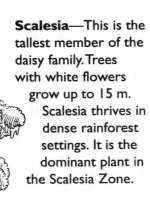

Scalesia—This is the tallest member of the daisy family. Trees with white flowers grow up to 15 m. Scalesia thrives in dense rainforest settings. It is the dominant plant in the Scalesia Zone.

Miconia—This flowering shrub grows 2–5 m tall. Its green leaves turn red-orange during the dry season. Clusters of flowers grow at the tips of the branches. Its fruit is a blue-black berry. It is the dominant plant in the Miconia Zone.

Mosses and liverworts—There are about 90 species of moss and more than 100 species of liverworts in the Galápagos. Both can often be found covering trees in the moist highland zones (as shown here). Separately, mosses are more often found in the Scalesia Zone, and liverworts in the Miconia Zone.

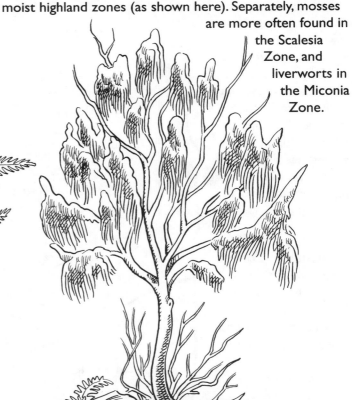

Ferns— Ninety different species grow in the islands, some as large as 3 m tall. They reproduce by spores, which can travel great distances. They grow in the Scalesia and Miconia Zones.

VEGETATIVE ZONES OF THE GALÁPAGOS

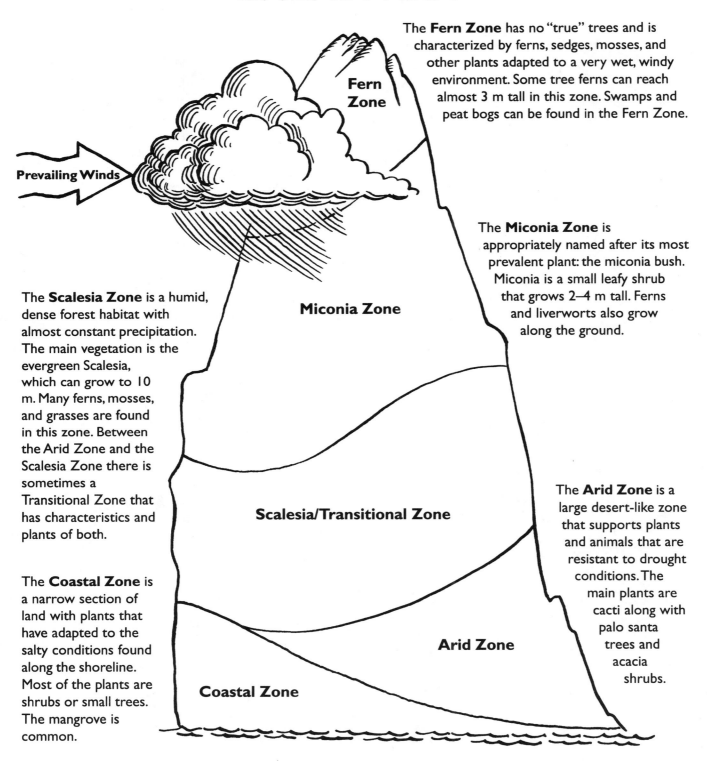

The **Fern Zone** has no "true" trees and is characterized by ferns, sedges, mosses, and other plants adapted to a very wet, windy environment. Some tree ferns can reach almost 3 m tall in this zone. Swamps and peat bogs can be found in the Fern Zone.

Fern Zone

Prevailing Winds

The **Miconia Zone** is appropriately named after its most prevalent plant: the miconia bush. Miconia is a small leafy shrub that grows 2–4 m tall. Ferns and liverworts also grow along the ground.

The **Scalesia Zone** is a humid, dense forest habitat with almost constant precipitation. The main vegetation is the evergreen Scalesia, which can grow to 10 m. Many ferns, mosses, and grasses are found in this zone. Between the Arid Zone and the Scalesia Zone there is sometimes a Transitional Zone that has characteristics and plants of both.

Miconia Zone

Scalesia/Transitional Zone

The **Arid Zone** is a large desert-like zone that supports plants and animals that are resistant to drought conditions. The main plants are cacti along with palo santa trees and acacia shrubs.

The **Coastal Zone** is a narrow section of land with plants that have adapted to the salty conditions found along the shoreline. Most of the plants are shrubs or small trees. The mangrove is common.

Arid Zone

Coastal Zone

CONSTRUCT YOUR OWN CLIMATOGRAMS

Create two climatograms, one for the Coastal Zone and one for the Fern Zone of Santa Cruz. Use the data of average temperatures and rainfall in the tables below. Then answer the following questions:

Coastal Zone—Rainfall and Air Temperature, Santa Cruz Island*

Months	J	F	M	A	M	J	J	A	S	O	N	D
Precipitation (cm)	4	2	0	22	22	1	2	2	3	4	2	3
Air Temp (°C)	24.6	26.2	27.3	26.8	26.3	24.8	23.9	23.2	22.7	22	23.6	24.5

*Data from Darwin Research Station

Fern Zone—Rainfall and Air Temperature, Santa Cruz Island*

Months	J	F	M	A	M	J	J	A	S	O	N	D
Precipitation (cm)	10	20	30	50	80	25	8	5	5	8	10	10
Air Temp (°C)	23	24.2	25.3	24.8	23.3	22.8	21.9	21.2	20.7	20	21.6	22.5

* Data approximate

1. Compare your climatogram of the Coastal Zone to that of the Fern Zone. How do precipitation and temperature change from zone to zone? Which weather factor is similar in both zones and which is different?

2. Within each zone, which weather factor is most consistent (stays the same)? Which factor fluctuates (changes) throughout the year?

3. The Galápagos Islands usually have two seasons: a wet season and a dry season. Using the climatograms, determine when the wet season begins and how long it lasts.

CONSTRUCT YOUR OWN CLIMATOGRAMS

4. Describe how you think plant and animal life might be affected by the wide variation in the amount of precipitation in the Galápagos. Would you expect plants and animals similar to those of the deserts of the American Southwest, or more like Florida or somewhere else? Explain your answer.

5. At the summits of the higher islands, water from the clouds that rest on the peaks condenses onto vegetation. How might this make the growing conditions different between the higher and lower elevations on these islands?

6. The prevailing wind causes the clouds (and the rain) to come from the south. How might this affect the size of the Arid Zone on the south side of Santa Cruz? On the north side?

7. What kinds of plants would you expect to find in the Arid Zone? In the Fern Zone?

BLANK CLIMATOGRAMS

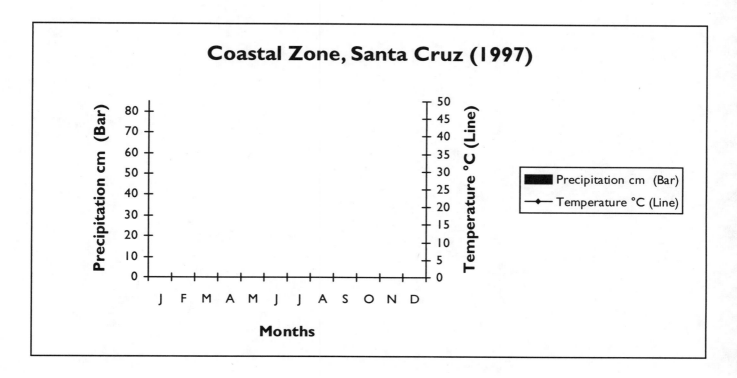

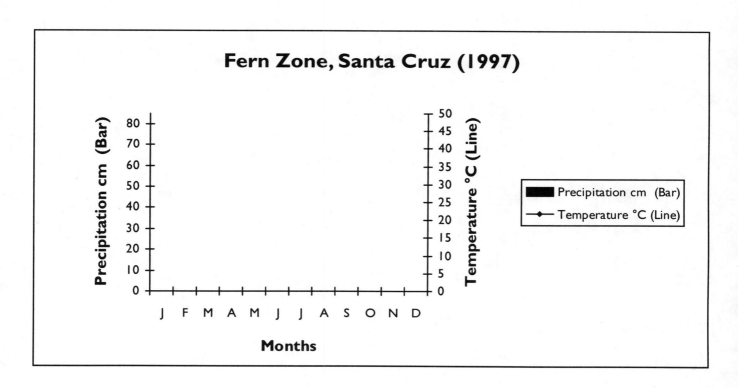

ARRIVAL OF LIFE

TEACHER SECTION
This activity is modified from a version created by NSTA for the Smithsonian Institution for the film *Galapagos in 3D*.

Background Information

I scarcely hesitate to affirm, that there must be in the whole archipelago at least two thousand craters—Nothing could be less inviting than the first appearance.

Charles Darwin, *Voyage of the Beagle*, 1845

Thus Darwin described the barrenness of some of the volcanic islands that are found in the Galápagos Island chain. The oldest Galápagos Islands formed several million years ago and have the greatest diversity of plants and animals. The young western islands of Isabela and Fernandina are active volcanoes and thus are still forming.

A volcanic island newly risen above sea level would be bare, rugged, and largely sterile. We can look at the Galápagos Islands as an example of how plants and animals arrive on newly formed islands and what conditions are necessary for their survival. We can investigate the wind patterns and ocean currents to find the mode of transportation for the pioneering plants and animals that came from the mainland and colonized the Galápagos Islands.

The Galápagos lie in a crossroads of wind and ocean currents that bring both cool (temperate-zone) and warm (tropical) water to the islands. Ocean currents brought an abundance of marine life that populated the islands' coastal waters. Wind currents brought birds, which fed on the rich marine life. Vegetation may also have been brought as windborne seeds and spores, or they may have been dropped by birds or on "rafts" of soil and plants. In more recent times, humans have brought more species, called *introduced* or *alien species,* to the islands, either intentionally (such as goats for food) or accidentally (rats that came on their ships). The problems associated with introduced species is explored in more detail in a later chapter.

The unusual cross-section of life on the Galápagos includes temperate-zone organisms, like the sea lion, and tropical organisms, like the butterfly fish. This mix is made possible by the converging currents and wind patterns.

Objective

- To create model experiments to see how seeds may have traveled from the mainland to the islands and still survive to germinate into plants.

Materials

The materials will vary depending on student creativity:

- Student handout:

  Modern-Day Darwins

- Various seeds (any seeds that are fast growing or easy to obtain, such as radish seeds, beans, sunflower seeds, grass seeds, etc.)

- Large container to hold enough salt water for the entire class

- Tap water

- Ocean water—if not available, use a solution of 35 g table salt (NaCl) per liter of water. ("Instant ocean mix" is sometimes available in pet supply stores.)

- Planting containers (pots, trays, etc.)

- Sterile (seedless) potting soil

- Materials to make simulated bird feet (straws, cotton swabs, tooth picks, etc.)

TEACHER SECTION

Although the Galápagos are unique because many of the plants and animals have evolved there and nowhere else, the islands are not unique in terms of the process of evolution. Evolution exists wherever life forms are found. Changes on isolated islands are sometimes easier to "see," but similar changes occur continuously throughout the living world.

Scientists think land rafts—floating logs and mats of root masses washed out from flooding rivers—are one way in which many of the terrestrial animals arrived at the Galápagos. In October 1995, 15 iguanas arrived on the eastern shore of the Caribbean island Anguilla. The group, including a pregnant female, traveled more than 320 km from the distant island of Guadeloupe on a land raft. Before this event there were no iguanas on the island, but they survived and reproduced, forming a new population.

Darwin's observations of the newness of some of the islands caused him to wonder how some of the organisms might have come to these "new" islands. During the years following Darwin's voyage on the *Beagle*, he worked on many projects relating to his observations. One topic that particularly fascinated him was how plants could have colonized the newly formed and relatively barren volcanic islands. Darwin conducted a series of experiments about seed dispersal to remote oceanic islands. In one experiment, Darwin found that out of 87 types of seeds, 64 germinated even after 28 days immersed in salt water, yet few survived immersion after 137 days.

In other experiments, Darwin investigated the possibility that seeds from the mainland were carried to the islands in mud stuck to the feet of birds that made their way to island landing sites. In one example, Darwin saved mud washed from the feet of a duck and germinated 53 plants from that mud. This has the same implication for humans, who may bring seeds or insects that travel on their shoes.

Procedure

Ask your students to devise a series of experiments to find out if seeds could survive the long salt-water journey in currents from mainland South America. This activity is best completed by research teams in small cooperative groups. Teams of three or four students will be able to conduct extensive research into how plants might have gotten to the Galápagos Islands. Students can be very creative, but some ideas include varying the time seeds can last in salt water, yet still be able to germinate, and studying seeds in the mud stuck to the feet of birds. One possible experiment is to mix seeds in potting soil and have students devise model "bird feet." Students can "walk" their model feet through the soil and try to harvest seeds from the attached mud.

Although you can provide a set of materials with which your students must work, you can also distribute the handout *Modern-Day Darwins* and have the teams discuss possible options, then bring in their own materials. This will provide a greater variety of results for your class to discuss.

Below are some questions students may ask during the course of their investigations. If students are having problems designing experiments, consider using some of these prompts:

- What seeds should we use?

- How long should we put the seeds in the "ocean"?

- How do we make model bird feet?

- How will my model bird "walk" in the mud?

- Where should we plant the seeds?

- How should we plant the seeds?

- How should we care for our newly planted seeds?

These discovery activities will help students understand the possible means of transport of plants that colonized the Galápagos Islands.

Standards

The material promoted in this activity enhances and supports student understanding of the following *National Science Education Standards* for grades 5–8:

Understandings about Scientific Inquiry (Science as Inquiry)

Different kinds of questions suggest different kinds of scientific investigations. Some investigations involve observing and describing objects, organisms, or events; some involve collecting specimens; some involve experiments; some involve seeking more information; some

TEACHER SECTION

involve discovery of new objects and phenomena; and some involve making models.

Science advances through legitimate skepticism. Asking questions and querying other scientists' explanations is part of scientific inquiry. Scientists evaluate the explanations proposed by other scientists by examining evidence, comparing evidence, identifying faulty reasoning, pointing out statements that go beyond the evidence, and suggesting alternative explanations for the same observations.

Scientific investigations sometimes result in new ideas and phenomena for study, generate new methods or procedures for an investigation, or develop new technologies to improve the collection of data. All of these results can lead to new investigations.

Diversity and Adaptations of Organisms (Life Science)

Biological evolution accounts for the diversity of species developed through gradual processes over many generations. Species acquire many of their unique characteristics through biological adaptation, which involves the selection of naturally occurring variations in populations. Biological adaptations include changes in structures, behaviors, or physiology that enhance survival and reproductive success in a particular environment.

Nature of Science (History and Nature of Science)

Scientists formulate and test their explanations of nature using observation, experiments, and theoretical and mathematical models. Although all scientific ideas are tentative and subject to change and improvement in principle, for most major ideas in science, there is much experimental and observational confirmation. Those ideas are not likely to change greatly in the future. Scientists change their ideas about nature when they encounter new experimental evidence that does not match their existing explanations.

It is part of scientific inquiry to evaluate the results of scientific investigations, experiments, observations, theoretical models, and the explanations proposed by other scientists. Evaluation includes reviewing the experimental procedures, examining the evidence, identifying faulty reasoning, pointing out statements that go beyond the evidence, and suggesting alternative explanations for the same observations. Although scientists may disagree about explanations of phenomena, about interpretations of data, or about the value of rival theories, they do agree that questioning, response to criticism, and open communication are integral to the process of science. As scientific knowledge evolves, major disagreements are eventually resolved through such interactions between scientists.

Assessment

Activity	Exemplary	Emergent	Deficient
	Students develop a testable hypothesis of how seeds could have colonized the newly formed Galápagos Islands. They are able to design and complete an experiment to test their hypothesis. Finally they are able to connect their results to their original hypothesis.	Students have some trouble coming up with a testable hypothesis. With some help they are able to complete their research.	Students have difficulty with developing a hypothesis and carrying out their experiments. They need help and direction throughout the activity and do not understand how organisms could have colonized the new Galápagos Islands.

MODERN-DAY DARWINS

After his trip to the Galápagos, Darwin wondered how plants got to the islands. Were they carried there by the ocean currents that travel from the coast of South America to the islands? Could seeds that fall into the ocean survive the saltwater? Could birds have brought seeds to the island and if so, how?

In the 1850s Darwin conducted experiments to test both of these hypotheses. Can you become a "modern-day" Darwin? Invent experiments to test whether seeds could travel ocean currents and survive the salt-water to take root on the distant barren islands. Create an experiment to test if birds may have carried seeds to the islands in the mud on their feet. Darwin collected birds from his own yard, washed mud off their feet, and then put the mud in a container to see if any plants sprouted. Simulate Darwin's experiment, but don't capture a flock of birds and wash their feet!

Procedure

1. Develop a hypothesis about how plants might have colonized the Galápagos Islands.

2. Design an experiment to test your hypothesis about how plants could have colonized the Galápagos. Make sure you use materials that are easily found, and show your experimental plan to your teacher for approval.

3. Conduct your experiment. Don't forget to keep detailed records of everything you do and observe, just as Darwin did during his experiments. Collect and record all your data, including weights, measurements, or counts, as necessary.

4. Analyze the results of your completed experiment and discuss them with your classmates.

5. Draw your conclusions. Have you come up with evidence to support how the barren Galápagos were populated by plants?

ISLAND BIODIVERSITY

TEACHER SECTION
This activity is modified from a version created by NSTA for the Smithsonian Institution for the film *Galapagos in 3D*.

Background Information

Remind your students of the location and the volcanic origin of the Galápagos Islands, and ask how a volcanic island newly built above sea level looks. After lava cools, eventually it becomes dark, black, basalt rocks (bare, rugged, and largely sterile). If you taught the previous activity, then your students should also be familiar with ideas of how vegetation arrived on the island—probably from seeds that were either blown by winds, floated by sea, or transported by animals from the mainland.

What conditions do plants need to grow? All plants need moisture and nourishment, and most need light, but plants vary greatly in their individual requirements. What growing conditions exist in the Galápagos? In an earlier activity students learned about the variation in the amount of precipitation found in each climate zone. Soil is thin in volcanic islands and relatively devoid of nutrients; rainfall is scant during most of the year, although there are better growing conditions in the highlands because of the increased moisture. Given this information, ask students whether they would expect to find a wide variety of plants surviving in these islands.

This concept should be familiar to your students if they have completed the activity *Climate Diversity*. This activity is an extension of that one and uses much of the same artwork and concepts. You may need to again review the water cycle with your students to help them understand how moisture is an intrinsic part of the environment, then distribute the handout *Vegetative Zones of the Galápagos*. Explain that rain is infrequent in the Galápagos, but as moist air brought by the prevailing winds from the south cools down, the result is misty precipitation high on the south sides of the island mountains. Just as with animals, different types of plant life adapt to different niches on a volcanic island. Plants are the basis of every terrestrial food chain, and this activity describes the dependence of vegetation on climatic conditions. The amount of biodiversity depends on the range of environments; the greater the range, the larger variety of plants, and thus a greater variety of animals that depend on the vegetation.

Objective

- To understand how climate and water cycles affect the local environment, and to form hypotheses about the effects of climate change on ecological zones and the species that inhabit them.

Materials

- Student handouts:

  Island Biodiversity

  Plant Species of the Galápagos (from activity 7)

  Vegetative Zones of the Galápagos (from activity 7)

- 11" x 14" (tabloid) paper
- Colored pencils
- Scissors
- Tape or glue
- Overhead projector (optional)
- Poster board (optional)

TEACHER SECTION

SCILINKS
THE WORLD'S A CLICK AWAY

Topic: biodiversity

Go to: www.scilinks.org

Code: EE90A

Topic: niches and habitats

Go to: www.scilinks.org

Code: EE90B

Procedure

Before class, copy and enlarge the handout *Vegetative Zones of the Galápagos* onto 11" x 14" (tabloid) paper. If this is not an option, you can use an overhead projector and poster board to trace an enlarged version of the island zones.

Divide your class into pairs and distribute the enlarged copies and the student handout *Plant Species of the Galápagos*. Give students time to read the descriptions of the plants, then have them color them, cut them out, and glue or tape them in the appropriate zone on the island picture.

Distribute the *Island Biodiversity* worksheet, allowing pairs time to answer each question. Discuss the concepts of moisture-dependent zones, the water cycle, and the effect of currents. Later activities will focus on El Niño and food webs, but these questions will introduce the idea that responding to environmental change is neither easy nor does it affect just one species.

Answers to student questions:

1. What factors are important in determining the type of vegetation that lives in each zone?

Moisture level, elevation, and amount of wind are key concepts.

2. What difference would you expect to find in the plants on the north side as compared with the south side of an island? Why?

The north side will have larger Arid Zones, and the more humid zones will begin at higher elevations. Because the south side gets more moisture from the prevailing winds, the humid zones will begin at lower elevations, and the Arid Zone will be much smaller, if it exists at all.

3. An El Niño or La Niña event can make big changes to the normal weather pattern of an island. During an El Niño the islands might face an unusually dry year. What might happen to the plants in each zone?

In the arid zone, there won't be much change because the plants are used to going without water. Humid zone plants that require a lot of moisture will suffer and possibly die out if the drought is long enough. In the case of a La Niña, where there is an abundance of rainfall, the arid zone plants will suffer. During recent La Niña events, visitors could see cactus "trees" that had fallen over because their roots had rotted from the excess moisture and could not support their own body weight.

4. In addition to the plants, what else might be affected by having an unusually dry year? Why?

> The animals that are adapted to eat those plants will be affected by losing a major source of food. They may also be affected if they are adapted to a moist climate (e.g., skin that easily dries out) or need to drink a lot of water directly.

5. What type of adaptations do plants such as cacti have for arid climates?

> They have thick skin to protect the water they keep in their body column.

6. List some of the adaptations plants might need for survival in the Arid and the Fern Zones.

> Arid Zone plants must store water for long periods and protect that water from animals that may want to eat or drink it (e.g., spines on a cactus). Fern Zone plants need to be able to repel large quantities of moisture from their leaves, and their roots do not rot in excessively moist ground.

7. The island shown here is 900 m high. Supposing it were only 300 m high, what kind of vegetation would grow in its top-most zone?

> The plants that grow in the Scalesia and Transitional Zones. The goal of this question is to show that not each island has all of the zones. Lower elevation islands will not simply have "smaller" areas of each zone, they may have only the Coastal and Arid Zones.

Standards

The material promoted in this activity enhances and supports student understanding of the following *National Science Education Standards* for grades 5–8:

Populations and Ecosystems (Life Science)

> A population consists of all individuals of a species that occur together at a given place and time. All populations living together and the physical factors with which they interact compose an ecosystem.

> The number of organisms an ecosystem can support depends on the resources available and abiotic factors, such as quantity of light and water, range of temperatures, and soil composition. Given adequate biotic and abiotic resources and no disease or predators, populations

TEACHER SECTION

(including humans) increase at rapid rates. Lack of resources and other factors, such as predation and climate, limit the growth of populations in specific niches in the ecosystem.

Diversity and Adaptations of Organisms (Life Science)

Biological evolution accounts for the diversity of species developed through gradual processes over many generations. Species acquire many of their unique characteristics through biological adaptation, which involves the selection of naturally occurring variations in populations. Biological adaptations include changes in structures, behaviors, or physiology that enhance survival and reproductive success in a particular environment.

Assessment

Activity	Exemplary	Emergent	Deficient
	Students are able to locate the correct zone for each plant described. They demonstrate a thorough understanding of the relationship between climate and vegetative zones. The students describe how weather changes might influence the plants and animals in various zones.	Students are able to locate the correct zone for most of the plants described. They understand the basic connections between climate and plant type, but have trouble describing how weather changes might affect plants and animals.	Students do not understand the connection between climate and vegetative zones.

ISLAND BIODIVERSITY

Procedure

With your partner, collect the materials from your teacher. On the handout *Plant Species of the Galápagos*, color in the plants, cut them out, and tape or glue the plants to their appropriate areas on the *Vegetative Zones of the Galápagos* handout.

Answer the following questions:

1. What factors are important in determining the type of vegetation that lives in each zone?

2. What difference would you expect to find in the plants on the north side compared with those on the south side of an island? Why?

3. An El Niño or La Niña event can make big changes to the normal weather pattern of an island. During an El Niño the islands might face an unusually dry year. What might happen to the plants in each zone?

ISLAND BIODIVERSITY

4. In addition to the plants, what else might be affected by having an unusually dry year? Why?

5. What type of adaptations do plants such as cacti have for arid climates?

6. List some of the adaptations plants might need for survival in the Arid and the Fern Zones.

7. The island shown on the *Vegetative Zones of the Galápagos* handout is 900 m high. Supposing it were only 300 m high, what kind of vegetation would grow in its top-most zone?

GALÁPAGOS MARINE FOOD WEB

TEACHER SECTION
This activity is modified from a version created by NSTA for the Smithsonian Institution for the film *Galapagos in 3D*. An online adaptation of this activity can be found at http://pubs.nsta.org/galapagos/.

Background Information

The main concept of this section is the flow of energy through an ecosystem. The procedures below will help familiarize students with the basic ecological concepts needed to understand this concept.

The trophic level that an organism occupies refers to where the organism gets its energy. Food webs may be divided into trophic levels; all the organisms in a particular trophic level are the same number of steps away from the primary producers on the lowest—or first—level. In most ecosystems, the first level of a food web is composed entirely of *producers*—organisms such as plants that get their energy directly from the sun. In some ecosystems there is a different energy source, such as thermal vents in the deep oceans. Organisms in trophic level two are those that feed on (and therefore get their energy from) the producers in level one. Organisms in trophic level three acquire their energy from those on level two; level four from level three, and so on.

Whereas the organisms in trophic level one are producers, the higher levels of a food web are composed of *consumers*—organisms that get their energy by eating other organisms. *Herbivores* occupy the second trophic level, getting their energy by eating producers. *Carnivores* and *omnivores* occupy the third level, getting their energy by eating herbivores. Carnivores and omnivores that eat other carnivores and omnivores occupy the higher levels. Students will need to understand this concept of energy flow to construct their marine food web.

Decomposers exist at all levels of a food web. They obtain their energy by devouring the dead organisms from every trophic level. Whether breaking down dead plants into the inorganic nutrients that make up the soils, or decomposing dead animals, decomposers are as important in a food web as all of the other organisms. Decomposers help to replenish the nutrients that are essential to the producers and help to rid the ecosystem of dead organisms that would quickly pile up.

Objectives

- To understand how food webs illustrate the ways in which organisms depend on each other for energy and nutrients.

- To make food webs showing the feeding relationships among organisms encountered in the Galápagos coastal waters.

Materials

- Student handouts:

    What's in a Food Web?

    Galápagos Marine Organisms

- Chart paper for posters

- Colored pencils, pens, or crayons

- Transparent tape or glue

- Overhead projector (optional)

TEACHER SECTION

SCiLINKS
THE WORLD'S A CLICK AWAY

Topic: producers
Go to: www.scilinks.org
Code: EE96A

Topic: consumers
Go to: www.scilinks.org
Code: EE96B

Topic: decomposers
Go to: www.scilinks.org
Code: EE96C

Each ecosystem has its own food web. This activity focuses on a food web for the marine ecosystem in the coastal waters of the Galápagos Islands. The ecology of a marine food web is influenced by environmental factors such as the climate, the salinity of the water, the ocean currents, and the winds. The procedures below will help you direct student discussions about many of these environmental influences.

After this activity is complete, as a further extension, you can have students create a food web of local organisms. They can use organisms found in their own back yards or organisms that are known to be from their region. Have students discuss their local food web in small groups using many of the same questions they encountered when discussing the Galápagos marine food web.

Procedure

Explain the difference between a food chain and a food web using the organisms of the Galápagos as examples. Two examples of simple food chains are given below. Write these on the chalkboard, or photocopy the images to compare with the food web. Explain to students that the arrows point in the direction of food (energy) flow. Point out also that in the first example, the turtle obtains its food from seaweeds that grow attached to rocks in shallow coastal areas. In the second example, small fish obtain their food from plankton, the floating algae, and tiny animals that drift in the water. In both cases, the first element of the food chain is a producer that converted light energy from the sun into chemical energy.

Compare these examples of simple food chains (below) with a more complex food web. Be sure students understand that a food chain shows relationships between specific organisms, while a food web shows interconnections among all the organisms in the same ecosystem.

Example Food Chains

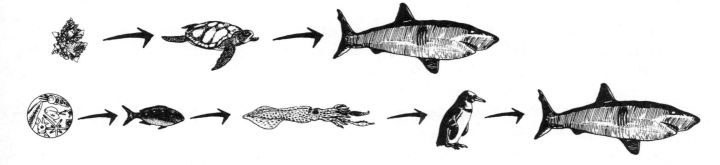

Example Food Web

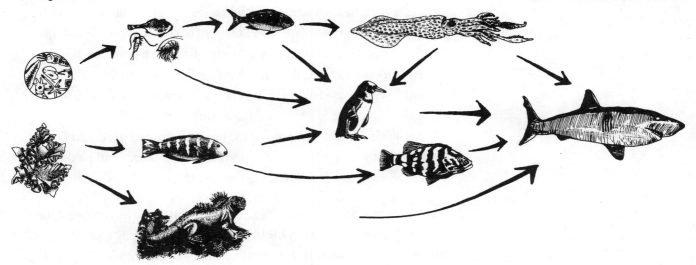

Build a class discussion around how environmental changes, even small ones, can have radical effects on an entire food web. Below are four examples of how environmental changes can have severe consequences for life in the Galápagos. Use these examples with your class to elaborate how a food web is dependent on many different factors. The questions on the *What's in a Food Web?* worksheet require students to understand these examples.

El Niño:

Marine iguanas primarily eat ulva, a type of green algae that looks like lettuce (a producer in trophic level one), which grows on rocks in the cool, shallow waters around the islands. What might happen to the marine iguana if, during an El Niño, the ocean temperatures were to rise and the ulva disappear? Because other types of algae are not as nutritious for the iguanas, they would suffer from malnutrition and weaken, probably dying from disease and predation before they would die of hunger. Marine birds such as penguins and flightless cormorants would also be adversely affected by a lack of food.

La Niña:

La Niña is a cold-water event that is opposite of the more famous, warm-water El Niño. Instead of causing increased rain, La Niña causes drought in the Galápagos. It also lowers the surrounding ocean temperature, causing species such as ulva to thrive. Marine iguanas would also thrive, because their food is so plentiful. (Although after the drought is over

Topic: food chain/food web

Go to: www.scilinks.org

Code: EE97A

Topic: trophic levels

Go to: www.scilinks.org

Code: EE97B

TEACHER SECTION

and the ulva populations reduce, the marine iguanas would once again starve because their numbers would be too great for the amount of ulva that can survive in normal conditions.) The cold water of the La Niña has an adverse effect on the warm-water fish that live in the Galápagos. In normal conditions, the warm Panama Current from the north brings with it a great diversity of marine fauna—almost half of the fish species of the islands come from the Central American, Colombian, and Ecuadorian coasts. But because the Galápagos waters are colder during La Niña, these species do not stay, and this lack of prey and predators severely affects all the species in the food web.

These examples demonstrate that an environmental change can cause some species to suffer and possibly die out if the change lasts long enough. However, there are other options besides simply dying out when environmental changes persist. A species may adapt to the new environment by using different food sources or new sources not found before the environmental change. Or, a species may move to a different location altogether and use the food sources there. Be sure to emphasize, however, that neither individuals nor species as a whole decide or "choose" to adapt (mechanisms of adaptation will be discussed in a later chapter). This can be a difficult concept for students at this stage.

Part A

Distribute copies of the student handouts *What's in a Food Web?* worksheet and *Galápagos Marine Organisms*. Although students should answer the worksheet after the food webs are completed, the questions will provide points to think about while working on the project. When the activity is completed, keep the students' posters hanging where they can continue using them for later activities.

Working either individually or in groups, students use the drawings in the handout *Galápagos Marine Organisms* to create a poster, bulletin board, or mural of a Galápagos food web. Students can color the pictures, cut them out, and tape or glue them onto their poster or mural to produce an accurate representation of a Galápagos food web. Recommend that your students lay out all the images before taping them down. Students will make another food web using the same organisms in a later activity, so you may want to make two copies of all the handouts. In this case, students can color and cut out everything now and save one copy for later. You can also use an overhead projector and poster board to trace enlarged versions of the drawings.

Note that the drawings provided are not to scale. Approximate sizes are included in most descriptions if you wish your students to calculate size ratios. Many descriptions indicate a predator, prey, or communal relationship with another organism. However, in some cases students will have to make connections based on general descriptions. For example, the description of the squid does not explicitly state it eats anthias fish, the description says it eats schooling fish. The description of anthias fish notes they travel in schools. Because scavengers, cannibals, and decomposers are difficult to include with arrows, you may want to have these species marked with a star or some other system of designation.

You can extend this project in many directions by having students research detailed information on the organisms provided, by researching additional organisms that may be in this food web, or by creating a comparable food web for their local environment or some other habitat they have recently studied. In the first activity of this book, *Where in the World?*, students were asked to select a city approximately 1,000 km from their own. Students can build food webs comparing organisms in this city to that of their hometown.

Part B

Have students answer the questions on *What's in a Food Web? worksheet*. Build a class discussion around the completed food web posters and the answers to the questions. Ask students to point out examples of producer and consumer species, herbivores and carnivores, and other examples from concepts discussed above.

Answers to student questions:

1. At which trophic levels of the food web would you expect to find the largest population (the total number of individuals of a particular organism)? The smallest population? Why might this be the case?

Populations are largest in trophic level one, at the bottom of the food web, and grow smaller with each successive level. Thus, the algae comprise the largest population, and the top carnivores (trophic level six) are the smallest population. The more a species is preyed upon, the lower its survival rate. Therefore, most species in this position have adapted to reproduce great numbers of offspring, with little energy put

ACTIVITY 10: GALÁPAGOS MARINE FOOD WEB

TEACHER SECTION

into raising them. Species that have few predators will produce fewer offspring and spend a greater amount of energy raising each.

2. *Which organisms might be described as "top carnivores" and why?*
Any organism that is not preyed upon is a top carnivore. The killer whale, Galápagos shark, and Galápagos hawk are all examples of top carnivores in this food web.

3. *How might changes in the environment affect populations of organisms? Below are two scenarios of environmental change. Give an example of how each of these might affect the food web.*
  • *El Niño: During an El Niño, there is less rainfall on land, and the water temperature around the islands rises.*
  • *La Niña: During a La Niña, there is increased rainfall on land, and the water temperature around the islands drops.*

See earlier in the Procedure section for more information.

4. *Make a list of organisms in your food web that live on land but are adapted to feed in the ocean. How has each adapted for feeding from the ocean? (Note that not all of these adaptations are the result of living in the Galápagos, because the forces that affect adaptation are in effect everywhere.)*

• Flightless cormorants developed powerful swimming legs but lost the ability to use their wings for flying.

• Marine iguanas developed a flattened tail to use like a rudder while swimming and a flattened snout to eat ulva, a lettuce-like algae that grows underwater on rocks. Their claws adapted for grasping the algae, and they have developed a system for excreting the excess salt they ingest by blowing it out of their snout.

• Penguins in the Galápagos, like all penguins, use their wings to swim in water rather than fly. There tends to be less food in warmer waters than in cold, so the Galápagos penguins are smaller than those found in the polar regions. Not only do they need less food to survive, but they also need less stored body fat to insulate them, as they are not swimming in freezing polar water.

• Sea turtles use their feet to paddle in the water rather than walk on land as do other turtles.

• Sea lions are mammals that have developed flippers as front and rear limbs, ideal for moving through water and serviceable for what little land-traveling they do. Their snout can be closed to keep water from getting into their lungs, and they have developed sleek, trimlined bodies for swimming quickly and capturing fish.

5. The Galápagos sea lion and fur seal are usually found in temperate or subtropical (cooler) waters. How do you think they have adapted to the warmer Galápagos climate? Specifically, think about how the warmer climate might have affected their feeding habits.

The sea lions and fur seals that live in Antarctic waters developed the ability to store more layers of body fat than those in warmer climates. They can acquire fat more easily than the animals in the Galápagos because food is generally more plentiful in cold waters than in the warmer Galápagos waters. With less food available, the Galápagos sea lions must eat often, so they enter the ocean to hunt more frequently. In another adaptation, milk from the Galápagos sea lion mothers contains less fat than milk from cold-water sea lions and fur seals. As a result, the Galápagos pups develop more slowly and are dependent on their mothers for nutrients much longer than their colder-water counterparts.

Standards

The material promoted in this activity enhances and supports student understanding of the following *National Science Education Standards* for grades 5–8:

Populations and Ecosystems (Life Science)

Populations of organisms can be categorized by the function they serve in an ecosystem. Plants and some microorganisms are producers—they make their own food. All animals, including humans, are consumers, which obtain food by eating other organisms. Decomposers, primarily bacteria and fungi, are consumers that use waste materials and dead organisms for food. Food webs identify the relationships among producers, consumers, and decomposers in an ecosystem.

For ecosystems, the major source of energy is sunlight. Energy entering ecosystems as sunlight is transferred by producers into chemical energy through photosynthesis. That energy then passes from organism to organism in food webs.

TEACHER SECTION

The number of organisms an ecosystem can support depends on the resources available and abiotic factors, such as quantity of light and water, range of temperatures, and soil composition. Given adequate biotic and abiotic resources and no disease or predators, populations (including humans) increase at rapid rates. Lack of resources and other factors, such as predation and climate, limit the growth of populations in specific niches in the ecosystem.

Structure of the Earth System (Earth and Space Science)

Global patterns of atmospheric movement influence local weather. Oceans have a major effect on climate, because water in the oceans holds a large amount of heat.

Assessment

Activity	Exemplary	Emergent	Deficient
Part A	Students are able to correctly describe and create the marine food web of the Galápagos Islands.	Students can make a partial marine food web, but do not correctly place all the organisms.	Students cannot create an accurate food web of the Galápagos marine environment.
Part B	Students discuss the marine food web accurately and are able to discuss all the class questions with a thorough understanding.	Students understand the structure of a marine food web, but do not understand how changes in the environment might influence the food web. They have trouble with some of the classroom questions.	Students have difficulty discussing the marine food web and do not add to the classroom discussion.
Extension	Students gather enough information about local organisms to create a complex food web. They can discuss the class questions in relation to their local food web.	Students make a local food web, but have trouble discussing it.	Students are not able to make a local food web and cannot discuss it.

WHAT'S IN A FOOD WEB?

1. At which tropic levels of the food web would you expect to find the largest population (the total number of individuals of a particular organism)? The smallest population? Why might this be the case?

2. Which organisms might be described as "top carnivores" and why?

3. How might changes in the environment affect populations of organisms? Below are two scenarios of environmental change. Give an example of how each of these might affect the food web.

    During an El Niño, there is less rainfall on land, and the water temperature around the islands will rise significantly.

    During a La Niña, there is increased rainfall on land, and the water temperature around the islands will drop.

ACTIVITY 10: GALÁPAGOS MARINE FOOD WEB

WHAT'S IN A FOOD WEB?

4. Make a list of organisms in your food web that live on land, but are adapted to feed in the ocean. How has each adapted for feeding from the ocean? (Not all of these adaptations are the result of living in the Galápagos, because the forces that affect adaptation are in effect everywhere.)

5. The Galápagos sea lion and fur seal are usually found in temperate or subtropical (cooler) waters. How do you think they have adapted to the warmer Galápagos climate? Specifically, think about how the warmer climate might have affected their feeding habits.

GALÁPAGOS MARINE ORGANISMS

TROPHIC LEVEL 6

Killer whales can reach lengths of 6.5 m. They are toothed whales that eat fur seals, sea lions, dolphins, young humpback whales, and large and medium-sized fish. Killer whales have no natural enemies. Their population size is limited by disease and food supply.

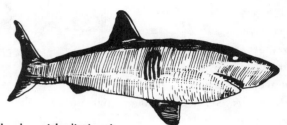

Galápagos sharks are large gray sharks with distinctive uniform coloration and reach 3 to 4 m in length. Their triangular upper teeth are sharp and serrated like steak knives. To satisfy their large appetites, they eat medium- to large-sized fish, and sometimes eat sea lions, fur seals, sea turtles, flightless cormorants, and occasionally marine iguanas. When human divers are in the water the sharks are very curious and approach them at close range, but usually are not aggressive. A large adult shark can be twice the size of a human diver. Only other large sharks (including cannibalistic members of their own species) prey upon them.

TROPHIC LEVEL 5

Bottlenose dolphins got their name because of their short, protruding snouts. As mammals, they must come to the surface to breathe air. Bottlenose dolphins are sociable animals, traveling in pods of about six or seven. Adults grow to approximately 2.5 m and feed on fish and squid. Their streamlined bodies allow them to swim at about 10 knots, darting in short bursts of speed to almost 20 knots. Killer whales prey upon the dolphins.

Fur seals found in the Galápagos are the smallest of all known fur seal species. Adult males grow to approximately 2.5 m and weigh about 70 kg; females are smaller, averaging about 35 kg. They live in colonies on rocks with shaded overhangs that protect them from the daytime sun, and there they breed and give birth. At night fur seals feed offshore, diving to about 30 m to catch fish and squid. Sharks and killer whales eat fur seals.

ACTIVITY 10: GALÁPAGOS MARINE FOOD WEB

GALÁPAGOS MARINE ORGANISMS

TROPHIC LEVEL 5

Sea lions are larger than fur seals, growing to almost 3 m. Sea lions spend their days in the water to stay cool. They feed both day and night, diving to depths of 200 m to catch fish. Adults are aggressive toward humans, but juveniles are playful and curious. Sharks and killer whales prey upon them.

Galápagos hawks belong to the category of birds known as raptors: birds of prey. Their feathers vary in color from white and brown to a brilliant yellow and black, and they may have a wingspan of nearly 1.5 m. Aided by their keen eyes, they are the principal native predator in the islands. In addition to land animals such as marine iguanas, they also eat the young of other seabirds, such as boobies and flightless cormorants. Galápagos hawks are also scavengers, feeding on virtually any dead animal. These birds have no native natural enemies.

TROPHIC LEVEL 4

Squid are bottom-dwelling carnivores that, like octopi, can change the color of their skin to blend in with their surroundings. Squid are also known for their ability to squirt a potential predator with "ink" and escape backwards by forcing water from a siphon near the head. Unlike their octopus relatives, squid are not solitary creatures. They swim in schools and will frequently follow the schools of fish on which they feed. Shark, fur seals, sea lions, and sea birds such as penguins prey upon squid.

The **octopus** is a bottom dweller that, in the Galápagos, can grow to about 30 cm. They can change color quickly to blend with the background and are difficult to see. Their untidy dens are easy to locate, however, because they leave empty seashells strewn about after eating. They eat small fish, crabs, and shellfish. Octopi are eaten by cormorants and groupers.

Groupers can grow to more than 1 m in length. They prey upon small and medium-sized fish, crabs, and crustaceans such as shrimp and lobsters. Groupers are eaten by sharks.

GALÁPAGOS MARINE ORGANISMS

TROPHIC LEVEL 4

Hieroglyphic hawkfish feed on small fish and crustaceans such as Sally Lightfoot crabs. They are medium-sized, shy creatures that tend to hide in coral reefs. From the coral, they use their pectoral fins to "sit up" and watch for prey. When they spot their prey, they swoop down and devour it quickly. The name *hawkfish* comes from this swooping hunting behavior. These hawkfish are blue-black with a camouflage of bluish stripes and brownish bands that look like hieroglyphics.

Galápagos penguins, which grow to about 36 cm tall, nest in holes along the shoreline. They cannot fly in the air, but seem to "fly" in the water using their greatly modified wings like paddles. Their swift underwater swimming allows them to catch small schooling fish. Food supply regulates the population of penguins in the Galápagos; when schooling fish or crustaceans are scarce, juvenile penguins cannot survive. Occasionally penguins are eaten by sharks, fur seals, and sea lions, but most die of starvation.

Blue-footed boobies are excellent fliers that feed on fish from the near-shore waters to a few km offshore. They frequently catch fish by folding their wings and diving down into the ocean from great heights. Their nests are on land, and hawks prey upon the chicks. When offshore fish are scarce, many young chicks die from lack of food. The adults are harassed by the frigate bird, which tries to steal their fish.

Flightless cormorants have very small wings and cannot fly, but they have thick, muscular legs adapted for swimming. They chase and catch octopus and small schooling fish that live within 10–15 m from shore. Like the boobies, they nest on land, and hawks prey upon their chicks. If the adult cormorant cannot find enough food, their chicks die. Sharks sometimes prey upon the adults.

Frigate birds, when fully grown, are about 1 m long with a 2 m wingspan, but weigh only a little over 1 kg. The frigate bird can use its long, pointed wings and forked tail to make sharp spiral turns and dive at great speeds through the air. Because of their habit of stealing fish caught by boobies and other birds, these graceful birds are sometimes described as parasites. They occasionally do their own fishing, however. Their population size is regulated by food supply.

GALÁPAGOS MARINE ORGANISMS

TROPHIC LEVEL 3

Humbpack whales are toothless baleen whales. They gulp in huge quantities of seawater, using baleen plates in their mouths to strain out zooplankton and small fish for food. Humpbacks winter in subtropical waters, where they breed, and summer in cooler waters. They prefer coastal waters and shallow banks. When they travel from summer to winter grounds, they swim in herds led by a large male. The humpback can grow to 15 m in length and weigh more than 900 kg. The killer whale is its natural enemy, preying upon its young.

Triggerfish have characteristic dorsal spines. When a triggerfish is chased into a rock or reef crevice by a larger, predatory fish, it opens its spines to wedge itself in place. The open spines not only make it difficult for the predator to dislodge the triggerfish, but also make the prey painful to swallow. Triggerfish eat sea urchins, algae, coral, crabs, and starfish.

Red-lipped batfish have broad, flat heads and slim bodies and are covered with hard lumps and spines. They grow to approximately 36 cm

long and are characterized by their vivid red lips. Batfishes are poor swimmers. Instead of swimming, they usually use their thickened, limb-like fins to walk on the sandy bottom. Batfishes have a long "snout" with whitish bumps. They use this bumpy protrusion as "bait" to catch prey such as small fish, small mollusks, clams, and worms.

Anchovies and **sardines** are small fish that normally live in the open ocean. They feed on zooplankton. When the zooplankton drift close to shore, these fish follow their food into shallow waters. Anchovies and sardines are food for some large fish species, penguins, and boobies.

GALÁPAGOS MARINE ORGANISMS

TROPHIC LEVEL 3

Sea turtles are air-breathing reptiles that come ashore to reproduce, but spend most of their lives at sea. They feed in shallow coastal waters, foraging for ulva, but also eating jellyfish and crustaceans. They sometimes migrate great distances in search of ulva beds. Like marine iguanas, green turtles starve when ulva becomes scarce during an El Niño event. Sharks prey upon green turtles.

Barnacles cement themselves tightly to rocks on wave-pounded shores; sometimes they attach themselves to living whales. By attaching themselves to whales, they are easily transported to new food areas. Barnacles are small, ranging from 1 to 3 cm in diameter. The barnacle's hard outer shell is made up of overlapping calcium plates around a central opening, which can be closed tightly to protect their soft inner parts. Barnacles feed by extending appendages out of their shell and waving them about to trap small animals and fragments of food; they filter zooplankton and small food particles from the water. Birds prey on barnacles.

Coral polyps, organisms that look like tiny sea anemones, secrete a hard, calcareous skeleton. Coral reefs are made up of colonies of corals. In the Galápagos, a coral head can be as small as a golf ball or as large as a house. Coral polyps use their tentacles to reach out and capture zooplankton for food. Symbiotic algae, called *Zooxanthelae*, live in the tissue of the polyps and benefit the coral by producing additional food as well as oxygen for the polyps to use. One type of sea urchin and a number of fish feed upon the coral polyps.

Sea anemones are entirely soft-bodied animals that attach themselves to rocks. They resemble flowers or miniature palm trees because of the circle of waving tentacles that surrounds their central stalk. Anemones have a symbiotic relationship with juvenile damselfish. They live within the anemone's tentacles, which offer protection to the fish. The damselfish's bright colors attract other fish to the anemone, which it then kills. The anemone and the damselfish both eat the captured prey. Anemones are active carnivores that wave their tentacles to attract and capture zooplankton. Fully extended, anemones in the Galápagos reach 6 cm in height and 3 cm in diameter.

GALÁPAGOS MARINE ORGANISMS

TROPHIC LEVEL 2

Marine iguanas live on the rocky shores, but dive in the near-shore water to depths of about 10 m to dine on the green seaweed ulva. When the ulva become scarce after an El Niño event, the marine iguanas try eating ceramium. Many iguanas starve because the ceramium does not fulfill their nutritional needs. Galápagos hawks prey upon marine iguanas on land, and occasionally sharks eat them in the water.

Sally Lightfoot crabs, so named because of their speed and agility, live on shoreline rocks both above water and to depths of about 1 m. Their flat bodies are well adapted to living in a high wave area. These small crabs feed on algae and in turn are eaten by some birds and fish. Adults are bright red, but the black color of the juveniles provides them somewhat greater protection from predators.

Parrotfish, so named because of its blue-green color and parrot-like beak, grows up to 1 m in length. It uses its beak to bite off and crush chunks of coral from reefs. Parrotfish are herbivores because although they "eat" coral, in fact  they only digest the algae coating on the coral, passing the broken remains of the coral through their digestive systems. They also eat ulva and ceramium. Despite their powerful beaks, they are gentle fish and creatures of habit that swim in schools along set feeding routes. They are food for larger predatory fish and sharks.

Damselfish grow 7–25 cm long and are sometimes described as "algal gardeners" because of the way they stake out and defend their home territories. The males chase away other herbivorous fish, including other damselfish. They also pick up herbivorous sea urchins and move them away from the algal mats. They eat different types of algae including ulva and ceramium. Juvenile damselfish have a symbiotic relationship with sea anemones, and they use the 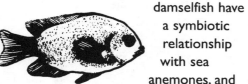 anemones' tentacles to protect themselves from their predators: larger fish and seabirds.

Sea stars and **sea urchins**, relatives of the crab, move about in large numbers over the submerged rocks and corals, searching for coral polyps and attached algae, such as ceramium, to eat. Sea stars have five rays (arms) arranged around a central mouth that is located on its underside. Tube feet help them hold onto rocks and move about in the water. Calcareous algae are their preferred food. Sea urchins have thick spines encasing and protecting their bodies. Like sea stars, they have mouths on the underside and tube feet. Predatory fish, such as triggerfish, eat both.

GALÁPAGOS MARINE ORGANISMS

TROPHIC LEVEL 2

Surgeonfish, notable for their beautiful color, grow to 25 cm in length and have one or two sharp spines on their sides. They swim together in small schools, aggressively chasing other herbivorous fish away from their territory. They feed on algae within a set area and predatory fish eat them.

Five-spotted anthias are small gray fish with up to five white spots on the side. They travel in large schools and feed on plankton. They are eaten by other fish, squid, or birds such as the penguin or flightless cormorant.

Zooplankton are animals that float or swim very weakly. Some zooplankton, like copepods, krill, and some jellyfish, remain as floating plankton all their lives. Others, like tiny **fish larvae**, eventually outgrow their early planktonic stage. As they drift, the zooplankton feed on phytoplankton and other zooplankton. Zooplankton are eaten by many organisms from higher trophic levels.

Copepods, at approximately 0.5–2 mm in length, are a smaller relative of crabs and lobsters and the most abundant group among marine **zooplankton**. The copepods found in the Galápagos are parasites that feed on the host tissue of almost every major animal group, including sponges, corals, fish, and mammals. Copepods, in turn, are a food source for many species of fish that eat zooplankton.

Krill are shrimp-like **zooplankton** that range in size from 8 to 60 mm. Most are bioluminescent (emit light), making them visible at night. These planktonic crustaceans feed on phytoplankton. They are a primary food source for penguins and are also eaten by various fish, birds, and whales.

While adult **jellyfish** in the Galápagos range in diameter from about 2 to 40 cm (though some species are considerably larger, with diameters of up to 2 m), until they reach their adult size, juvenile jellyfish are microscopic and sometimes considered part of **zooplankton** because they are microscopic, free-floating animals. Some jellyfish filter-feed on phytoplankton and zooplankton, while others eat small fish that they catch in their tentacles. The tentacles have stinging cells (nematocysts) that poison and paralyze captured prey. Large fish and sea turtles feed on jellyfish.

TEACHER SECTION

Ulva is a fast-growing green algae found from the shoreline to depths of about 8–10 m. When fully grown, ulva looks like seaweed or loosely arranged lettuce leaves; it is often called "sea lettuce." Ulva is the favorite food of the marine iguana and an important food for turtles, as well as for damselfish and many other herbivorous fish. Thus ulva is usually found in the Galápagos looking more like mowed grass than like lettuce. The herbivores keep it cropped to about 2 cm. Warm water and a lack of nutrients during the El Niño almost wiped out the ulva population, depriving many herbivores of their primary food.

Sargassum is a brown seaweed averaging about 15 cm in length. It has characteristic air sacs that support it in the water. Although it is abundant, many organisms do not eat it because it contains toxic substances.

Phytoplankton are the very abundant but tiny (less than 1 mm) algae and plant-like organisms that drift in the ocean. Phytoplankton live near the surface, using sunlight, carbon dioxide, and water to produce food and oxygen. When they are deprived of nutrients, however, as they are in El Niño years, their numbers decrease, affecting the entire food web. Phytoplankton provide food for zooplankton and other, larger, organisms.

Ceramium is a small (5 mm) filamentous red algae that provides food for damselfish, surgeonfish, parrotfish, some sea stars, and snails. When ulva are almost wiped out by an El Niño, marine iguanas start eating ceramium, but these red algae do not provide all the nutrients the iguanas need.

EL NIÑO AND ISLANDS

Background Information

This activity builds upon ones earlier in the book, including *Climate Diversity* and *Galápagos Marine Food Web*. If you have not completed the *Climate Diversity* activity, you will need to familiarize your students on how to graph a climatogram. If you have not completed the *Galápagos Marine Food Web*, you will need to skip that portion of this activity.

Students need to be familiar with the climatic phenomena known as El Niño or ENSO (El Niño Southern Oscillation) in order to understand how it influences entire populations of organisms. El Niño is a disruption of the ocean/atmospheric system in the tropical Pacific that has important consequences for weather around the world. The National Oceanographic and Atmospheric Administration (NOAA) defines El Niño as a weather pattern characterized by a large-scale weakening of the trade winds, and warming of the surface layers in the eastern and central equatorial Pacific Ocean. El Niño events occur irregularly at intervals of two to seven years, although the average is about once every three to four years. Because of its isolation, and the fact that it is surrounded by water, an island is more radically affected by an El Niño than is a large continent.

When an El Niño event occurs, warm ocean currents appear on the Pacific coast of South America during the summer. The unusually warm water affects the Galápagos marine ecosystem, and any organism that is a part of the complex food web will be influenced by the changes this warm water brings.

In addition to unusually warm ocean water, the amount of rainfall increases, and the air temperature rises. The increased rainfall affects the terrestrial ecosystems of the islands, because more rain usually means better growing conditions for land plants and more food for most land animals.

Students will learn about the many effects of El Niño on islands by reading *El Niño and the Galápagos*, adapted from materials by NOAA and a report

Objective

- To understand the El Niño phenomena and the importance of the abiotic—non-living—environment on communities of organisms, both in the Galápagos and throughout the world.

Materials

- Student handouts:

    Effects of El Niño

    El Niño and the Galápagos

    Galápagos Marine Organisms (from activity 10)

TEACHER SECTION

Topic: el niño

Go to: www.scilinks.org

Code: EE114

prepared by the scientists at the Charles Darwin Research Station, located on Santa Cruz Island. From this reading they will learn about the causes of El Niño as well as about some of the results of the 1982–83 El Niño—one of the most dramatic in history. The report includes graphs of air and water temperatures and precipitation from the past 30 years. For more information on El Niño and the Galápagos, visit the Charles Darwin Research Station Web site: http://www.darwinfoundation.org/NewFiles/news/newsindex.html.

Procedure

Distribute copies of the handouts *Effects of El Niño* and *El Niño and the Galápagos*. Because the reading is long, you may wish to assign this as homework. This activity requires good reading comprehension, so you may want to go over the reading first and make a glossary list of words your students may find difficult to understand.

Part A

After students read the handouts, they make a list identifying which years an El Niño event occurred. This activity forces students to read the article and tables and pick out the necessary information to make the list. The table below has data of El Niño years from the entire twentieth century, even though this section focuses only on the last 30 years.

El Niño Years

1902–03	1905–06	1911–12	1914–15	1918–19
1923–24	1925–26	1930–31	1932–33	1939–40
1941–42	1951–52	1953–54	1957–58	1965–66
1969–70	1972–73	1976–77	1982–83	1986–87
1991–92	1994–95	1997–98		

Part B   **TEACHER SECTION**

Students create two climatograms, comparing an El Niño year and a "normal" year. They should correctly graph the climatograms and realize that 1997 is an El Niño year because of the increased rainfall and water temperature.

Below are answer keys to the climatograms:

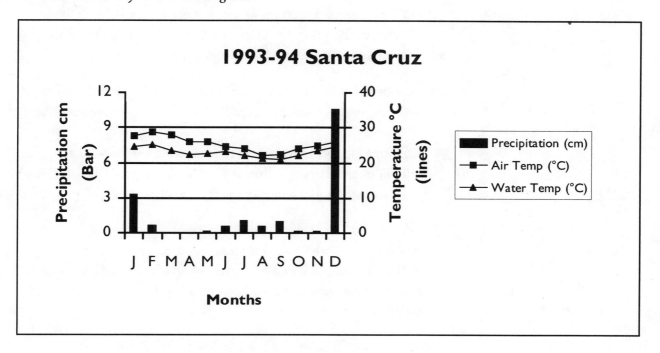

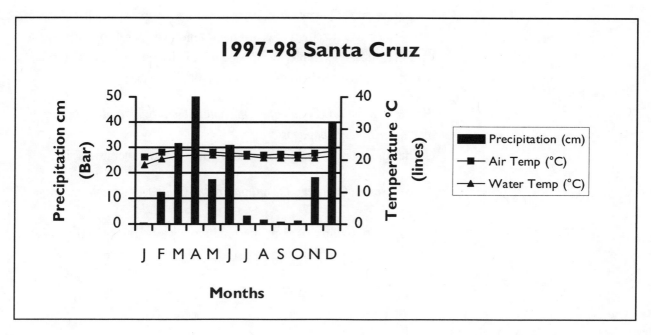

TEACHER SECTION

Part C

Answers to student questions:

1. What is an El Niño, and how often do they occur?

An El Niño is a global weather or climate event that affects populations of organisms and ecosystems in many areas of the Earth. El Niño is a disruption of the ocean/atmospheric system in the tropical Pacific that has important consequences for weather around the globe. El Niño events occur irregularly at intervals of two to 10 years, although the average is about once every three to four years.

2. Give examples of how the El Niño event described affected the California as opposed to the northern states between the Rocky Mountains and the Great Lakes?

California experienced increased rainfall, which led to flooding, mudslides, and damage to lives and property. In contrast, the northern states from the Rocky Mountains to the Great Lakes enjoyed a very mild winter.

3. How did the El Niño of 1982–83 affect Ecuador and Peru?

In Ecuador and northern Peru, up to 250 cm of rain fell during a six-month period, transforming the coastal desert into a grassland dotted with lakes.

4. What is a La Niña event, and how is it different from El Niño?

La Niña causes below-normal ocean surface temperatures in the eastern equatorial Pacific; therefore, its effects tend to be nearly opposite those of El Niño. For example, El Niño led to massive flooding in California, and La Niña led to below-normal rainfall in the same area.

5. How does a typical El Niño affect the amount of rainfall and the water temperature in the Galápagos?

The amount of rainfall increases and the ocean temperatures rise.

6. Explain some of the ways the animals of the Galápagos are affected by an El Niño.

Animals of Galápagos were affected in many ways by the El Niño event of 1982–83. Some birds and marine mammals, as well as marine iguanas, suffered severe decreases in their populations, mainly due to the following factors:

- death, caused especially by the absence of food and increased illness
- reproductive failure, probably related to lack of food
- migration to other locations

7. Compare the effects the El Niño had on birds that feed on marine life, compared to birds that feed on land animals or plants.

While birds that rely on marine life were devastated by El Niño, because the change in water temperatures affected their ability to live in the region, populations of land birds exploded because the additional rain increased their food supply.

8. What are some effects of the El Niño on the plants in the Galápagos?

Plant populations exploded in what are usually arid areas, and there was unusually rapid and abundant growth in the highlands of some islands. Changes in the vegetation varied according to the life zone (ecosystem) and type of plants present. Generally, species in the arid zones reacted with much greater speed to the increased rainfall. Herbs and climbing plants especially expanded very rapidly, with increased germination of seeds that had been dormant in the soil for months or years. However, notable death occurred among adult individuals of the giant cacti and large *Scalesia* trees, which could not support their own weight when their roots rotted due to excessive rainfall.

Part D

Students take the data from *El Niño and the Galápagos* and create new marine food webs, reflecting the changes brought by an El Niño, as described in the readings. This food web should be different from the one completed in the *Galápagos Marine Food Web* activity because of the changed environment. For example, the reading indicates that Galápagos penguins suffered a 78% population decrease. This will affect the organisms that prey upon them, as well as the organisms they feed upon. The reading lists only some of the marine animals used in the earlier food web activity, so the students will have to apply these affects to the other organisms.

Standards

The material promoted in this activity enhances and supports student understanding of the following *National Science Education Standards* for grades 5–8:

Populations and Ecosystems (Life Science)

A population consists of all individuals of a species that occur together at a given place and time. All populations living together and the physical factors with which they interact compose an ecosystem.

The number of organisms an ecosystem can support depends on the resources available and abiotic factors, such as quantity of light and water, range of temperatures, and soil composition. Given adequate biotic and abiotic resources and no disease or predators, populations (including humans) increase at rapid rates. Lack of resources and other factors, such as predation and climate, limit the growth of populations in specific niches in the ecosystem.

Structure of the Earth System (Earth and Space Science)

Water, which covers the majority of the Earth's surface, circulates through the crust, oceans, and atmosphere in what is known as the "water cycle." Water evaporates from Earth's surface, rises and cools as it moves to higher elevations, condenses as rain or snow, and falls to the surface where it collects in lakes, oceans, soil, and in rocks underground.

Global patterns of atmospheric movement influence local weather. Oceans have a major effect on climate, because water in the oceans holds a large amount of heat.

Assessment

Activity	Exemplary	Emergent	Deficient
Part A	Students are able to list all nine El Niño events, based on the readings.	Students have some difficulty listing all nine El Niño events, based on the readings.	Students can list few or no El Niño events, based on the readings.
Part B	Students are able to accurately graph the climatic data of El Niño and "normal" years. Students can easily explain the differences between normal and El Niño events.	Students have trouble graphing the climate data without coaching. The graphs lack detail or proper labels. Students have some difficulty explaining an El Niño event.	Students cannot graph the climate data. They do not know what kind of graph to make, or their graphs are incorrect. Students cannot explain an El Niño event.
Part C	Students are able to pull the correct information from the readings to answer the questions.	Students have difficulty answering the questions, or their answers are only partially correct.	Students cannot pull the necessary information from the readings or answer the questions.
Part D	Students construct a food web that reflects the ecological changes resulting from an El Niño event.	Students need extra coaching to construct an accurate web that reflects the ecological changes resulting from an El Niño event.	Students cannot use the El Niño data to create a food web that might result from this event.

EFFECTS OF EL NIÑO

An El Niño is a global weather or climate event that affects populations of organisms and ecosystems in many areas of the Earth. El Niño is a disruption of the ocean/ atmospheric system in the tropical Pacific that has important consequences for weather around the globe. El Niño events occur irregularly at intervals of two to 10 years, although the average is about once every three to four years.

Your first task is to read about the El Niño weather patterns that affect many parts of the world and to complete the directions and questions below. The readings are long, so you may want to make notes or underline important points so you can easily find them later.

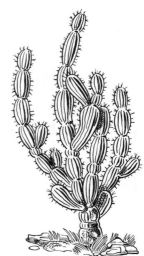

Part A

Read the handout *El Niño and the Galápagos*. Using the data recorded over the last 30 years, make a list identifying which years an El Niño event occurred. Remember, an El Niño year is characterized by increased rainfall, warmer air temperatures, and higher water temperatures. (Hint: There are nine identified El Niño years between 1965 and 1998.)

Part B

On a piece of graph paper, using the data below from the years 1993–94 and 1997–98, make two climatograms. If possible, align the two graphs on the same piece of paper. Which of these two years do you think is an El Niño year, and why?

1993–94, Santa Cruz Island

Months	J	F	M	A	M	J	J	A	S	O	N	D
Rain (cm)	3.3	.7	0.0	0.0	.2	.6	1.1	.6	1.0	.2	.2	10.6
Air Temp (°C)	27.6	28.7	27.9	25.9	26.0	24.5	24.0	22.2	22.3	23.9	24.8	26.0
Water Temp (°C)	24.6	25.2	23.5	22.3	22.5	23.1	22.1	21.3	21.0	22.1	23.5	24.5

1996–97, Santa Cruz Island

Months	J	F	M	A	M	J	J	A	S	O	N	D
Rain (cm)	.4	9.7	25.3	40.1	13.7	24.7	2.4	1.2	.5	.8	14.6	31.7
Air Temp (°C)	26.1	28.2	29.0	28.7	28.1	27.8	27.5	27.1	27.2	26.9	27.6	28.6
Water Temp (°C)	23.0	25.3	26.7	27.1	27.0	26.7	26.4	25.9	25.8	25.8	25.9	26.6

EFFECTS OF EL NIÑO

Part C

On a separate sheet of paper, answer the questions below based on what you've read about El Niño.

1. What is an El Niño, and how often do they occur?

2. Give examples of how the El Niño event described affected the California as opposed to the northern states between the Rocky Mountains and the Great Lakes?

3. How did the El Niño of 1982–83 affect Ecuador and Peru?

4. What is a La Niña event, and how is it different from El Niño?

5. How does a typical El Niño affect the amount of rainfall and the water temperature in the Galápagos?

6. Explain some of the ways the animals of the Galápagos are affected by an El Niño.

7. Compare the effects the El Niño had on birds that feed on marine life, compared to birds that feed on land animals or plants.

8. What are some effects of the El Niño on the plants in the Galápagos?

Part D

Now, using the data from the reading and the information from the *Galápagos Marine Food Web* activity you've already completed, you will construct another food web of the same Galápagos marine environment. This time, however, construct a food web as it would exist at the end of a severe El Niño event. Remember to use the information about how the plants and animals are affected by an El Niño to construct the food web.

EL NIÑO AND THE GALÁPAGOS

An example of the close relationship between the ocean and the atmosphere is seen in the climate events known as El Niño and La Niña. Scientists refer to these as ENSO—the El Niño Southern Oscillation.

In 1997–98, the world witnessed a major ENSO event. Near the equator, the eastern portion of the Pacific Ocean warmed from 5 °C to 9 °C above normal, resulting in changes to the jet streams in both the northern and southern hemispheres. The end results were floods or droughts throughout much of the world's mid-latitudes. California received increased precipitation (usually rainfall), which led to some flooding, mudslides, and damage to lives and property. In contrast, the northern states from the Rocky Mountains to the Great Lakes enjoyed a very mild winter—golf was played all year in Minnesota!

Weather Events

In normal years, the winds tend to blow from east to west across the Pacific, near the equator. The easterly winds push the surface waters westward across the ocean. In turn, this causes deeper, colder waters to rise to the surface. This *upwelling* of deep ocean waters brings with it the nutrients that otherwise would remain near the bottom. The fish populations living in the upper waters are dependent on these nutrients for survival. During El Niño years, however, the winds weaken, stopping the upwelling of the colder deep water. As the ocean warms, the warmer water shifts eastward, as do the clouds and thunderstorms that produce heavy rainfall along the equator. El Niño events occur every three to five years on average.

These events happen because the relationship between the ocean and the atmosphere is disturbed. Ocean surface temperatures have to increase only by 1 °C for jet streams to bring storms to normally dry regions and drought to humid regions.

El Niño's Effects Around the World

The 1982–83 El Niño was very strong. The presence of unusually warm ocean water and the atmospheric changes combine to produce an unusual increase in the quantity of rainfall along the coast of South America. In Ecuador and northern Peru, up to 250 cm of rain fell during a six-month period, changing the coastal South American desert into a grassland dotted with lakes. In coastal terrestrial ecosystems, such as in the Galápagos, this climate change has important impacts on ecosystems that are linked to the ocean. Unusual wind patterns also caused monsoon rains to fall over the central Pacific instead of its western edge, which led to droughts and terrible forest fires in Indonesia and Australia.

Overall, the loss to the world's economy as a result of El Niño amounted to more than $8 billion. Likewise, the record-breaking El Niño winter of 1997–98 resulted in unusual weather in many parts of the world. In the United States, severe weather events included flooding in the Southeast, major storms in the Northeast, and flooding in California.

EL NIÑO AND THE GALÁPAGOS

La Niña

By May 1998, the El Niño event was largely over, but rapid cooling in the eastern tropical Pacific led to a La Niña event. La Niña causes below-normal ocean surface temperatures in the eastern equatorial Pacific; therefore, its effects tend to be nearly opposite those of El Niño. For example, El Niño led to massive flooding in California, and La Niña led to below-normal rainfall in the same area.

A body of open ocean, some 1,240 km wide and 300 km from north to south, cooled by up to 10 °C in 30 days! Mother Nature demonstrates an enormous ability to adjust the thermostat of Planet Earth.

The Galápagos and the El Niño of 1982–83

In 1982–83, the El Niño was so strong that scientists named it "the event of the century." Large areas of the Ecuadorian coast suffered serious problems, including the loss of human life.

Graph 1. Rainfall in the Galápagos, 1965–98

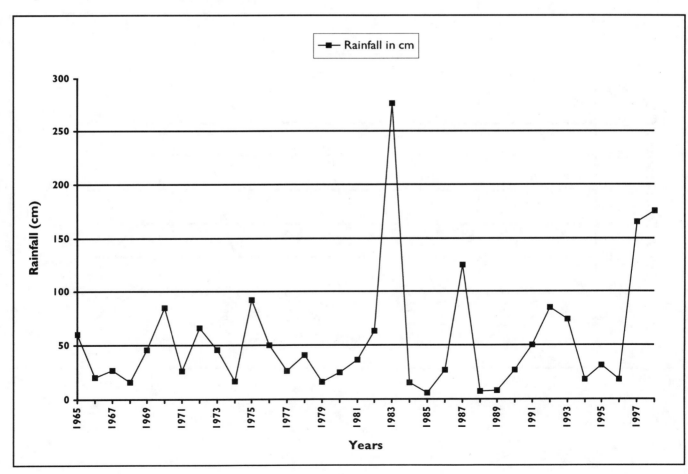

EL NIÑO AND THE GALÁPAGOS

The Galápagos Islands were no exception. In 1983 the weather station of the Charles Darwin Research Station registered 201 days with measurable rainfall, and total precipitation for 1983 was 276.9 cm. In normal years measurable rainfall occurs on only about 50 days in a year, and total yearly precipitation averages 38.5 cm. Graph 1 shows rainfall data from 1965 through 1998. The highest peak occurred in 1983 when El Niño reached its greatest intensity.

In 1983, the average monthly ocean temperature reached 28.6 °C in March, compared to normal years when the average temperature is 25.5 °C. Graph 2 shows average yearly ocean temperatures observed between 1965 and 1998. The high peak in 1983 is clearly visible and is the highest average yearly ocean temperature observed during more than 30 years of observations.

Graph 3 displays changes in average annual air temperature. Again, high temperatures peaked in 1983, with a yearly average of 25.7 °C, compared to a normal yearly average of 23.8 °C. The highest average air temperature occurred in March 1983, reaching 27.8 °C.

Graph 2. Ocean temperature in the Galápagos, 1965–98

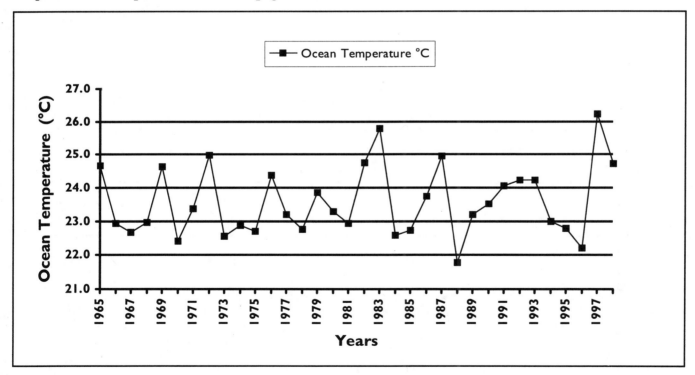

EL NIÑO AND THE GALÁPAGOS

Graph 3. Air temperature in the Galápagos, 1965–98

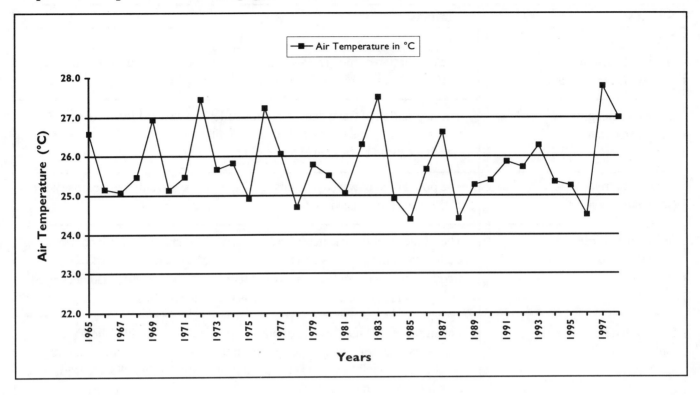

Fauna (animals)

The fauna of Galápagos was affected in many ways by the El Niño event of 1982–83. Some birds and marine mammals, as well as marine iguanas, suffered severe decreases in their populations, mainly due to the following factors:

- death, caused especially by the absence of food and increased illness
- reproductive failure, probably related to lack of food
- migration to other locations

The effect was easily seen in the colonies of blue-footed boobies on Española Island, in the nesting of waved albatross on the same island, and in the populations of flightless cormorants, Galápagos penguins, and marine iguanas throughout the islands. On the other hand, populations of land birds increased a great deal; for example, the Galápagos finches reproduced in great numbers due to the abundance of food on land. The table on the next page shows how the 1982–83 El Niño event affected some of the animals of the Galápagos.

EL NIÑO AND THE GALÁPAGOS

Effects of the 1982–83 El Niño event on the animals of the Galápagos

Species	Effects
Marine life	
Flightless cormorant (*Nannopterum harrisi*)	The population of the flightless cormorant suffered a 45% decrease. By the end of 1983, reproduction had begun again and evened out in 1984.
Galápagos penguin (*Spheniscus mendiculus*)	The population of Galápagos penguins suffered a 78% decrease. As of 1998 (15 years later!), the number of penguins still has not reached the population size that existed before the El Niño event.
Waved albatross (*Diomedea irrorata*)	The population of waved albatross on Española Island suffered because none of the birds reproduced.
Great frigatebird (*Fregata minor*)	The situation of the frigatebird colonies was different on each island. On Genovesa Island matings and nesting during March and April 1983 were frequent; in August of the same year, the percentage of nesting had decreased to 6.1%. On Española, however, no birds were seen nesting.
Blue-footed booby (*Sula nebouxii*)	The numbers of blue-footed boobies went down considerably. There was increased migration to other locations in the archipelago, but the death rate was high, especially around Fernandina Island. By October 1983, reproductive activity was again increasing.
Marine iguanas (*Amblyrhynchus cristatus*)	Populations of marine iguanas suffered death rates of 45–70%, depending on the location. Marine iguanas that survived had an average weight loss of 30% because they tried to replace their diet of ulva (which was no longer available due to the increased water temperatures) with ceramium, a species of algae they could not digest. After the most intensive phase of the El Niño event ended by August 1983, the populations of marine iguanas recovered rapidly.
Sea lions (*Zalophus californianus* and *Arctocephalus galapagoensis*)	Populations of sea lions suffered a general decrease throughout the islands for three main reasons: a) an increased death rate of young sea lions; b) increased amount of diseases; and c) migration to other locations.
Sharks (Class *Chondrichthyes*)	The Galápagos and Hammerhead sharks migrated to deeper locations in the ocean, where the water was colder. Other species of shark, usually found in warmer waters, moved into the area. These warm-water sharks prey on larger organisms in the marine ecosystem.

EL NIÑO AND THE GALÁPAGOS

Species	Effects
Whales and porpoises (Order *Cetacea*)	In general, an absence in whales and porpoises was observed; it was assumed that they migrated to areas where more food was available.
Groupers (Family *Serranidae*)	These warm-water fish increased in numbers because of the rise in water temperatures.
Life on Land	
AmberJacks (*Seriola dummerili*)	These warm-water fish increased in numbers because of the rise in water temperatures.
Dolphinfish (*Coryphaena hippurus*)	These warm-water fish are normally found in only the northern areas of the Galápagos Islands, but their numbers increased and they appeared in the southern areas as well.
Other marine animals	Changes occurred in the makeup of marine communities and number of various species. Although numbers of some species of fish lessened, other species (typical of warmer tropical waters) appeared. There was an increased death rate among corals.
Darwin's finches (Family *Fringillidae*)	The 1982-83 El Niño event gave rise to a big increase in the populations of various species of finches throughout the islands. The increase occurred because the birds nested more frequently, apparently due to the greater abundance of food. However, this increased reproductive success caused increased predation on chicks, especially by Galápagos mockingbirds.
Mockingbirds (*Nesomimus* spp.)	As in the case of the finches, populations of mockingbirds increased as a result of the El Niño event. However, the mockingbirds were more susceptible to heavy rains that destroyed mockingbird eggs and killed recently hatched chicks.
Land iguanas (*Conolophus* spp.)	There are no data on the reaction of land iguanas to the El Niño event of 1982-83. However, in the drought years that followed, populations suffered increased death rates.
Giant tortoises (*Geochelone elephantopus*)	The giant tortoises of Galápagos did not suffer noticeable changes. On Santa Cruz Island most giant tortoises migrated from the highlands toward the lowlands. Young tortoises grew more rapidly during the El Niño event than in normal years.

EL NIÑO AND THE GALÁPAGOS

Flora (plants)

Immediate effects of the El Niño event could be seen in the vegetation of the Galápagos Islands. Plant populations also increased in what are usually arid (dry) areas, and unusually quick and plentiful growth occurred in the highlands of some islands.

Changes in the vegetation varied according to the climate zone (ecosystem) and type of plants present. Generally, species of the arid zones reacted much more quickly to the increased rainfall. Herbs and climbing plants grew especially quickly. Similarly, increased germination (sprouting) occurred in seeds that had apparently been dormant (inactive) in the soil for several months or years. However, large numbers of adult giant cacti and *Scalesia* trees died because they could not support their own weight when their roots rotted due to all the rain.

Plants in the most humid zones were less sensitive to increased rainfall than were plants in the arid zone. As in the arid zones, humid zone species that benefited most from increased precipitation were herbs and climbers. Again, *Scalesia* suffered greatest death in adults more than 10 years old.

El Niño in 1997

In the Galápagos, the second half of 1997 was marked by unusual climate conditions, with patterns more similar to those expected early in the year rather than in July, August, or September. The year 1997 had strong rains during the first half of the year. The increased rainfall caused a large amount of water to be soaked into the ground, which caused the roots of many plants to rot. Large plants, such as the giant cacti and large *Scalesia* trees, fell over and died because their rotted roots could not support their own weight. The air temperature in 1997 was also above normal.

From the point of view of long-term conservation, one of the greatest concerns about an El Niño event is that it helps spread introduced species to the Galápagos, causing permanent ecological change.

TORTOISE TALES:
ECOLOGICAL RELATIONSHIPS

TEACHER SECTION
This activity is modified from a version created by NSTA for the Smithsonian Institution for the film *Galápagos in 3D*. An online adaptation of this activity can be found at http://pubs.nsta.org/galapagos/.

Background Information

This activity explores several of the important ecological relationships that make up a typical ecosystem. These community relationships help us identify the niche that each organism occupies in its habitat and also helps us identify and understand the interrelationships between and among organisms. The ecology of the Galápagos can be very complex because the pristine conditions that once existed in such a remote part of the world no longer prevail, thanks to human interference. The interrelationships of the native animals on the islands are greatly influenced by introduced species such as dogs, goats, rats, and pigs, as well as humans.

Students will be asked to interpret the different types of ecological relationships found with the giant tortoise. Apart from being an icon of the Galápagos, tortoises have been hunted nearly to extinction, then salvaged from extinction by humans. Details of human-tortoise interactions have been recorded for more than 300 years. The giant tortoise has been the subject of intense research by scientists at the Charles Darwin Research Center for more than 35 years, so much is known about the ecological relationships of the tortoise with other species.

This activity can tie in directly with the *Galápagos Marine Food Web* posters completed earlier. Examples and answers are provided with the definitions below. The handout *Local Ecological Relationships* chart provides an optional extension into the students' local environment.

Types of Ecological Relationships

Competition

Two or more organisms vie for the same food source or energy source. Competition can be *inter*-specific (between individuals of different species) or *intra*-specific (between individuals of the same species).

Objective

- To understand the concepts of *competition, predation, parasitism, mutualism,* and *commensalism* and apply them in a typical Galápagos Island community.

Materials

- Student handouts:

    Ecological Relationships

    Local Ecological Relationships (optional)

TEACHER SECTION

Topic: predation

Go to: www.scilinks.org

Code: EE130

Dr. Jackson's journal example: Tortoises compete with one another as well as with the wild goats for food.

***Galápagos Marine Food Web* activity example:** Various fish, sea turtles, and marine iguanas all eat ulva, so each competes with the others for food.

Predation

One organism (the predator) kills and consumes another (the prey) for food.

Dr. Jackson's journal example: Galápagos tortoises were killed for food by sailors and pirates in the nineteenth century.

***Galápagos Marine Food Web* activity example**: Sharks prey on turtles; larger fish eat smaller fish; many birds feed on fish.

Parasitism

One organism (the parasite) takes food from another (the host).

Dr. Jackson's journal example: Mites and ticks suck blood from the tortoise.

***Galápagos Marine Food Web* activity example:** Frigate birds steal the catch of other seabirds; copepods live in the tissue of host species.

Mutualism

A relationship involving two organisms in which both organisms benefit.

Dr. Jackson's journal example: The tortoise is "cleaned" of ticks and mites by the ground finches that eat these parasites for food (energy), and the tortoise benefits by not losing blood to the parasitic insects. Another example is that both the prickly-pear cactus and the Galápagos tomato provide food (energy) to the tortoise. The digestive system of the tortoise does not use the seeds of these plants, so they are eliminated. Because the outer covering was digested, the seeds are much more likely to germinate.

***Galápagos Marine Food Web* activity example:** Juvenile damselfish and sea anemones have a mutualistic relationship. Damselfish position themselves within the tentacles of the anemone, their bright colors luring prey for the anemone. Meanwhile, the anemone's stinging tentacles protect the damselfish from predators.

Commensalism

An ecological relationship in which one organism benefits and the other is not affected by the relationship.

Dr. Jackson's journal example: The scientists at the Darwin Research Station help tortoises survive by raising the endangered young in protected areas. Humans receive no benefit from this action.

Galápagos Marine Food Web **activity example:** When barnacles attach themselves to whales they do not hurt the whales (except for the possibility of slowing them down a little). The barnacles get free transportation to new food areas.

Procedure

Discuss the five types of ecological relationships listed above: competition, predation, parasitism, mutualism, and commensalism. Then divide the class into groups of four and distribute copies of the handout *Ecological Relationships,* which has a journal entry from fictional ecologist Dr. Betsy Jackson. Although fictional, the activities and observations described by Dr. Jackson are accurate, and the journal describes examples of the relationships covered in this activity.

For example, when Dr. Jackson writes in her journal

> "[t]he sailors would take many animals and stack them in the holds of their ships so they could have fresh food for months"

she is describing predation by humans on the tortoises.

Have each group of students read the journal, then fill in the final column as they discuss each ecological relationship described by Dr. Jackson. Have them list examples of each type of relationship, with the giant tortoise as one of the animals in each case. Alternatively, these ecological concepts can be introduced in the form of a research activity by having each group investigate these ecological relationships using the Internet or other reference materials.

ACTIVITY 12: TORTOISE TALES

TEACHER SECTION

The chart of *Local Ecological Relationships* is an optional extension that can be done either in class or as a homework assignment. Before asking students to fill in this chart you can reinforce the definitions of these relationships with the *Galápagos Marine Food Web* activity completed earlier. Point out, or have your students find, examples of each of these relationships with species shown in the food web. Finding examples on the poster will help students recognize similar relationships locally or in another environment they have studied. For variation in answers, you can have students each research ecological relationships in different habitats that they have been studying (desert, mountain, arctic, etc.). Have students work in groups to discuss the ecological relationships they discovered in their own backyard, parks, or local zoo.

Standards

The material promoted in this activity enhances and supports student understanding of the following *National Science Education Standards* for grades 5–8:

Populations and Ecosystems (Life Science)

A population consists of all individuals of a species that occur together at a given place and time. All populations living together and the physical factors with which they interact compose an ecosystem.

The number of organisms an ecosystem can support depends on the resources available and abiotic factors, such as quantity of light and water, range of temperatures, and soil composition. Given adequate biotic and abiotic resources and no disease or predators, populations (including humans) increase at rapid rates. Lack of resources and other factors, such as predation and climate, limit the growth of populations in specific niches in the ecosystem.

Assessment

Activity	Exemplary	Emergent	Deficient
	Students work in groups to completely fill in the correct ecological relationships described.	Students work in groups but need teacher coaching. They have difficulty finding all the correct relationships.	Students do not work successfully in student groups. They cannot find correct ecological relationships.

ECOLOGICAL RELATIONSHIPS

Dr. Betsy Jackson's Tortoise Observations

Betsy Jackson is a field researcher at the Darwin Research Station in the Galápagos Islands. She is researching the Galápagos giant tortoise, *Geochelone elephantopus,* and is trying to establish a detailed database of the ecological role of the tortoise on Española Island. Española is a small island located in the southern part of the Galápagos Archipelago. Below is one of her journal entries, which describes what she has observed.

July 23, 1999, Española Island

I've spotted the giant tortoises at last! These tortoises are of the saddleback variety; that is, they have an arched opening in their carapace (shell). I can easily see how their carapace's large neck-opening allows the turtles to reach the taller pads of the tree-like prickly-pear cactus. Apart from the pads of the cactus, the tortoises also seem to like the pear fruit from this species. I know from my research that eating the cactus pear is not only good for the tortoise, it is also good for the cactus itself. The seeds of the cactus are protected by a thick coating of fruit and can only sprout into new plants if the fruit has been eaten, digested, and the seeds eliminated by an animal. Both organisms benefit from this relationship: the tortoise benefits by getting sustenance from the fruit, and the plant benefits because its seeds now have a better chance of taking root and growing. This relationship is not unique to the prickly-pear cactus; it is also found in many other fruit-bearing plants, such as the Galápagos tomato.

As I observe the tortoises in the field, I notice that ground finches interact with the tortoises in a very interesting way. Quite frequently, I see a finch land on the giant tortoise and pick at the small bugs that are bothering it. The finch picks what looks like a mite or a tick from the tortoise and eats it. This way the finch gets some food and the tortoise is cleaned of many of the small parasites that seem to bother many island animals. The finch is not the only bird that interacts with the giant tortoise. Back in June I saw a young hawk perch on the back of a large male tortoise. The hawk was taking advantage of the perch to watch the fields for lava lizards, but the tortoise did not seem to be aware of the hawk's presence.

The tortoises do not run away from the other animals around them, including me! I can get extremely close to them without scaring them away. My background research on these tortoises indicates that this lack of fear is part of the reason their current population numbers are so low. The population was estimated at more than 250,000 individual tortoises before whalers, pirates, and even explorers over the centuries captured them by the thousands for food. Before modern technology made storing food for long periods easy, it was difficult for sailors to keep food on board without it going bad. Because the tortoise can go for long periods without water, sailors would take many animals and stack them in the holds of their ships so they could have fresh food for months. The current population of tortoises on the islands is only 15,000–20,000, but the numbers are improving.

ECOLOGICAL RELATIONSHIPS

Humans killing these animals is not the only reason their numbers decreased. As humans came to the islands, they brought with them dogs, goats, and pigs for food, and rats came ashore from their ships. The pigs and rats eat tortoise eggs, and dogs prey upon young turtles who can't move fast enough to escape. Although goats do not eat the tortoises themselves, they eat huge quantities of the lush vegetation that the tortoises need so desperately to survive.

The best part of my research is knowing that I will be helping the population of the tortoises increase in number. The scientists at the Darwin Research Station have been helping the Galápagos Tortoise by collecting unhatched eggs and hatching them in captivity so no other animals can eat them. After raising the young tortoises for two to three years, they are returned to the same island that the eggs came from. The tortoises benefit from this relationship, even though the scientists do not.

In the table below explain each ecological relationship listed by defining it and then giving one example of this relationship from Dr. Jackson's journal.

Relationship	Definition	Examples
Competition		
Predation		
Parasitism		
Mutualism		
Commensalism		

LOCAL ECOLOGICAL RELATIONSHIPS

Complete the chart below, using examples of ecological relationships of species found in your local environment or another habitat you have studied.

Ecological Relationship	Species 1	Species 2	Who Benefits
Competition			
1.			
2.			
3.			
Predation			
1.			
2.			
3.			
Parasitism			
1.			
2.			
3.			
Mutualism			
1.			
2.			
3.			
Commensalism			
1.			
2.			
3.			

THE TOMATO AND THE TORTOISE:
EXAMPLES OF COEVOLUTION

Background Information

Galápagos Islands ecosystems support many different kinds of relationships, several of which were covered in the *Tortoise Tales* activity (predation, parasitism, etc.). If you have not already completed that activity, you may wish to do so before conducting this one. This activity focuses on the mutualistic relationship between the giant tortoise (*Geochelone elephantopus*) and the Galápagos tomato (*Lycopersecon esculentum*) because the relationship also demonstrates coevolution.

Coevolution is an intertwining of adaptations and behaviors between two (or more) species living in a habitat. The interactions of the species may influence the adaptations of both species. True coevolution occurs when two or more species influence each other's evolution. Mutualism is actually an example of coadaptation, but it is thought that this mutual interdependence is usually the result of coevolution.

In many dry areas, plants develop thick, gelatinous seed coats to conserve the moisture inside the seed. Before such seeds can germinate, the seed coat must be cut, scratched, or softened in some way to allow water to enter. Only about one percent of the seeds of the Galápagos tomato will germinate under normal weather conditions. However, if a tortoise eats a tomato, the seeds will remain in the tortoise's stomach for up to three weeks while digestive acid (HCl) dissolves the gelatinous coating. When the seeds are expelled from the tortoise's digestive tract, they readily germinate. Thus, what appears to be only an herbivore eating a plant is actually a mutualistic relationship that benefits both organisms.

Another example of coevolution is on the island of Mauritius, off the east coast of Madagascar, the home of the now-extinct dodo bird. On Mauritius, the calvaria major tree once was abundant but declined in population over the last few hundred years—by the 1970s only 13 trees remained, all of which were more than 300 years old. The trees that remained still produced healthy-looking seeds, but none of them ever germinated.

Objectives
- To observe the effect of acid (HCl or weak acetic acid) on tomato seeds.
- To relate observations to interspecific relationships in organisms.
- To understand the concept of coevolution.

Materials
- Student handout:
    Life of a Tomato Seed
- Three small jars (baby food size) or waxed paper cups
- Three tomatoes cut into halves
- Tap water
- Dilute hydrochloric acid (0.1 mol) or vinegar mixed 1:1 to simulate stomach acid
- Safety goggles
- Paper towels
- Strainer
- Spoon
- Three plastic zipper bags with labels
- Graph paper
- Marking pens
- Pencils

ACTIVITY 13: THE TOMATO AND THE TORTOISE

Because the tree's fruit had been eaten by the dodo—a large bird with a gizzard filled with food-crushing stones—it has been suggested that the tree's seeds adapted to withstand this digestive crushing by developing a thick, tough seed coat. This seed coat was then worn down and possibly cracked, without damaging the seed itself, by the dodo's digestive system. When the digested seeds were subsequently eliminated by the dodo, they were in a condition to germinate quite easily. Seeds with very thick seed coats had a survival advantage over thinner-coated seeds—until the dodo went extinct almost 300 years ago.

Once the dodo became extinct, the calvaria could no longer germinate and therefore was doomed. Although the remaining trees kept producing seeds, without the coexistence of the dodo, the seeds could not germinate.

Students should be reminded that the environment—while acting as a selective force in the process of natural selection—includes other organisms in the ecosystem as well as abiotic factors such as temperature and rainfall. This activity will allow the students to simulate some of the interactions between plants and animals.

Procedure

Part A

Day 1

Divide the class into groups of three or four. On day 1, distribute the student handout *Life of a Tomato Seed*, tomatoes, jars or cups, spoons, and marking pens to each group. Place containers of water and diluted acid in a central location. Students should wear safety goggles when working with acid. Students should then follow the directions on the handout.

Day 2

At the beginning of the next class, supply each group with the rest of the materials and have them continue following directions on the handout.

Days 2–12

Over the next 10 days, students should check their bags to make sure their paper towels are still damp, and add water as necessary.

Part B

Day 12

After 10 days (ending day 12 from when the project started), distribute graph paper and ask students to answer the questions and create the graphs requested on their handout. Have one person from each group write the group total on the board, then have the students average the class data.

As an extension, try repeating these steps with other plant seeds to find out if they are affected in the same way. You can also experiment with the length of time allowed for soaking and sprouting. Record data under these variables and compare the results.

Answers to student questions:

1. What role does each environment (water, acid, and air) play in helping seeds to germinate? Give an example of a seed in each situation.

- Acid: Seeds in acid germinate the fastest because the acid dissolves the seed coating. This situation is similar to seeds that pass through the digestive system of an animal.

- Water: Seeds in water germinate more slowly than those in acid, but faster than those in the air, because water does penetrate the seed to some degree. This is similar to seeds that drop into a puddle or are rained upon.

- Air: Seeds in air will germinate the least because nothing has worked to dissolve their coating. This is similar to seeds that fall to the ground and are exposed to the air.

2. Which produces a higher rate of germination: acid or air?
Acid.

3. How does the water-only environment compare with the acidic or dry environments?
Water produces less germination than acid, but more than air.

4. Which of the three samples of seeds was most like the environment in a tortoise's digestive system and why?
The sample of acid-soaked seeds is most similar to those that have passed through the tortoise's digestive system because of the presence of stomach acid.

TEACHER SECTION

5. Do you think that animals help the seeds of other plants to sprout in a similar way?

> Yes, but only for those seeds that are adapted for this type of mechanism. Exposure to acid may destroy other types of seeds.

Standards

The material promoted in this activity enhances and supports student understanding of the following *National Science Education Standards* for grades 5–8:

Structure and Function in Living Systems (Life Science)

Living systems at all levels of organization demonstrate the complementary nature of structure and function. Important levels of organization for structure and function include cells, organs, tissues, organ systems, whole organisms, and ecosystems.

Reproduction and Heredity (Life Science)

Reproduction is a characteristic of all living systems; because no individual organism lives forever, reproduction is essential to the continuation of every species. Some organisms reproduce asexually. Other organisms reproduce sexually.

The characteristics of an organism can be described in terms of a combination of traits. Some traits are inherited and others result from interactions with the environment.

Diversity and Adaptations of Organisms (Life Science)

Biological evolution accounts for the diversity of species developed through gradual processes over many generations. Species acquire many of their unique characteristics through biological adaptation, which involves the selection of naturally occurring variations in populations. Biological adaptations include changes in structures, behaviors, or physiology that enhance survival and reproductive success in a particular environment.

Assessment

Activity	Exemplary	Emergent	Deficient
Part A	Students follow instructions completely and continually monitor their plants' growth. After completing the project, the students create an accurate bar graph and correctly calculate class averages.	Students follow instructions but do not monitor their plants regularly. They have difficulty calculating the percentages and creating a bar graph.	Students neither follow instructions nor monitor their plants regularly. They do not graph their data or calculate percentages.
Part B	Students are able to completely explain the relationship between the tomato activity and the growth of tomato plants in the Galápagos. They explain coevolution correctly.	Students need help explaining the relationship between the tomato activity and the growth of tomato plants in the Galápagos. They do not completely explain coevolution or seem to understand it entirely.	Students do not explain the activity correctly to the class and do not seem to understand the concept of coevolution at all.

LIFE OF A TOMATO SEED

In all ecosystems, one can observe many different types of relationships. This activity focuses on the mutualistic relationship between the giant Galápagos tortoise (*Geochelone elephantopus*) and the Galápagos tomato (*Lycopersecon esculentum*). This relationship is an example of coevolution, which occurs when two or more species influence each other's evolution. In many dry areas, plants develop thick, gelatinous seed coats to conserve the moisture inside the seed. Before such seeds can germinate, the seed coat must be cut, scratched, or softened in some way to allow water to enter. Only about one percent of the seeds of the Galápagos tomato will germinate under normal weather conditions. However, if a tortoise eats a tomato, the seeds will remain in the tortoise's stomach for up to three weeks while digestive acid (HCl) dissolves the gelatinous coating. When the seeds are expelled from the tortoise's digestive tract, they readily germinate. Thus, what appears to be only an herbivore eating a plant is actually a mutualistic relationship that benefits both organisms. We will simulate what happens to a tomato seed both when eaten by a tortoise and when not eaten by a tortoise.

Day 1

1. Label the first container "Water," the second "Acid," and the third "Air."

2. Use a spoon to scoop out the pulp and seeds of each half-tomato, and place the pulp in one of the cups or jars.

3. Cover the seeds and pulp in the first container with tap water. Cover the seeds and pulp in the second container with the diluted acid. Leave the seeds and pulp in the third container exposed to the air.

Day 2

1. Drain, rinse, and dry the seeds and return them to the labeled containers.

2. Count the number of seeds in each container and record the data in the "Number at Start" boxes on the data table on the next page.

3. Dampen one of the paper towels with water, spread the seeds from the first container on one side of the paper towel, and fold the towel over to cover the seeds.

4. Place the folded towel with the seeds in a zipper bag and label the outside of the bag to match the appropriate container: Water, Acid, or Air.

5. Repeat with the rest of the seeds.

ACTIVITY 13: THE TOMATO AND THE TORTOISE

LIFE OF A TOMATO SEED

Days 2–12

1. Group members should take turns every day for 10 days checking the bags to be sure that the towel is still damp, and adding water if necessary.

Day 12

1. After 10 days open the towels, count the seeds that have germinated, and record this data on your table below. Calculate the percentage of seeds in each container that germinated in the table below, and create a bar graph showing the differences for each bag.

2. Can you explain the relationship between the activity you have completed and the growth of tomato plants in the Galápagos? As a group, answer the following questions on a separate sheet of paper.

- What role does each environment (water, acid, and air) play in helping seeds to germinate? Give an example of a seed in each situation.

- Which produces a higher rate of germination, acid or air?

- How does the water-only environment compare with the acidic or dry environments?

- Which of the three samples of seeds was most like the environment in a tortoise's digestive system?

- Do you think that animals help the seeds of other plants to sprout in a similar way?

Each group will report its results to the rest of the class. After you have collected data from all the groups, add their data to your own, and construct a bar graph of the class results.

Team	Air		Water		Acid	
	Number at Start	Number Germinated	Number at Start	Number Germinated	Number at Start	Number Germinated
	Percent		Percent		Percent	

$$\frac{\text{Number of Seeds Germinated}}{\text{Number of Seeds at Start}} \times 100 = \text{\% Germinated}$$

THE PROBLEM OF INTRODUCED SPECIES

Background Information

Introduced or invasive species are organisms that have accidentally or purposefully been brought into an otherwise isolated environment. Of course, some introduced species are neither beneficial nor harmful to the new environment. Humans have introduced many species into local environments for agricultural purposes: crops, livestock, forestry, etc. However, when introduced plants or animals invade natural ecosystems and compete with *endemic* (native) species, the introduced species are called *invasive species*. And all environments are at risk from invasive organisms.

In North America, the purple loosestrife *(Lythrum salicaria)* is an invasive species because it has taken over many natural wetland ecosystems, driving out native species of plants and affecting the breeding success of waterfowl and reptiles. Another introduced species in North America is the European house sparrow *(Passer domesticus)*. In 1853, 50 house sparrows were brought from Europe to Brooklyn, New York. By the early twentieth century the house sparrow was widely dispersed across Canada, the United States, and Mexico. Whether or not the house sparrow is invasive is open to interpretation.

Because island ecosystems are isolated and smaller than continental ecosystems, invasive species can have a far greater impact in a shorter period of time. Organisms that evolve in isolated island environments have limited natural competitors. When invasive species are introduced, they are often able to out-compete the native species by preying directly on the endemic organisms, by competing with them for the same food, by damaging their nesting sites, or by reproducing faster. Native species can be forced into extinction by the more successful newcomers. Although similar scenarios occur in nature as an ordinary part of natural selection, when humans are the cause of the introduction, this is no longer natural selection but artificial interference in the environment.

Objectives

- To learn how an introduced species can directly or indirectly affect an island's ecology.

Materials

- Student handout:
    Introduced Goats vs. Giant Tortoises
- Paper
- Pencils
- 30 m of twine
- Paper plates
- Chairs
- Whistle (or other signaling mechanism)
- Several blindfolds

ACTIVITY 14: THE PROBLEM OF INTRODUCED SPECIES

TEACHER SECTION

Now that humans live in a global society with access to almost every corner of the world, introduced species are appearing almost everywhere. The problems associated with introduced species are just now being realized, because delicate environments are increasingly being destroyed. The activities below focus on the Galápagos, but the problem of introduced species is everywhere.

Some of the unique animals that live in the Galápagos are threatened by new species that have been introduced to the area. This lesson graphically demonstrates the impact of introduced species and illustrates the very specific habitat requirements of some species.

Explain to students that when a new type of living thing is brought into an ecosystem, it directly or indirectly affects all the other creatures in that system. On many of the Galápagos Islands, packs of wild dogs have killed great numbers of young marine iguanas, sea birds, fur seals, and penguins—a direct negative impact on the endemic species. On some of the islands goats roam freely. They were introduced on San Salvador as early as 1813 by the captain of a ship from the United States. On other islands, fishing expeditions and early settlers brought goats as a source of meat and milk. This activity will illustrate the impact of goats on the Galápagos ecosystem; the two parts will show that a single introduced species, such as goats, can affect a wide range of endemic species, such as giant tortoises or tiny ground finches.

Procedure

Part A

Introduce the concept of habitat destruction as a threat to living things. Elicit from students' experience some examples of how people have changed the environment and eliminated species. (Paving prevents plant growth; draining marshes drives away waterfowl and fish, etc.) Then discuss the different ways an introduced species can affect an ecosystem.

Give students copies of *Introduced Goats vs. Giant Tortoises*, which uses a journal entry from Dr. Jackson to introduce the concept of introduced species. Divide the class into partners and ask each pair to read and discuss the problem of goats on Isabela Island.

ACTIVITY 14: THE PROBLEM OF INTRODUCED SPECIES

Your students have already done one or more food webs in earlier activities, now ask them to create food webs involving the Galápagos tortoise, both before and after the introduction of goats to the islands. Have each team create a concept web or some other drawing that shows the relationship of the goats to the tortoises on Isabela. Finally, have each team make a drawing of what an ecosystem on the island of Isabela might have looked like before the introduction of goats and what it might look like after their introduction. Be sure to suggest that they include tortoises in both drawings. Discuss the finished drawings before going on to Part B.

Part B

Make arrangements to use the gym or an outdoor playing field when you teach this lesson. This activity is similar to musical chairs. As an option, you can assign a student to record the rates of habitat destruction in each round.

In Part A, students learned how goats have a negative effect on the Galápagos tortoise. In this activity, they will learn how goats affect Galápagos finches.

1. Take the class to an open area such as the gym or the schoolyard. On the ground or the gym floor, lay out 30 m of twine to form a circle representing the island. In the circle, place 10 chairs to represent trees or bushes and 10 paper plates randomly on the ground to represent ground finch nests. Explain that while some Galápagos finches nest in vegetation, with several nests in any one tree, ground finches build nests on the ground, each a meter or so away from another.

2. Divide the class into two groups, with one student separate from the rest. Blindfold the single student and explain that he or she will represent a goat. Students in one of the groups will represent ground finches, while the other group will be finches that nest in trees. Each night, the ground finches must return to their paper plate nests and the other finches to their chair nests. Have the "finches" enter the circle and mingle for about 30 seconds. Sound a whistle, at which time all the finches must find nests. A ground nest (paper plate) can be occupied by only one bird, but a tree (chair) can house two birds (they need to touch the chair to be "safe," but they do not both have to sit on it). There should be enough nest sites for all students in this first round. (For example, if you have 25 students in your class, in the first round you will need 12

TEACHER SECTION

paper plates and six chairs.) Signal the whistle again to indicate that students should leave their nests to begin foraging.

3. Direct the blindfolded "goat" to walk slowly through the habitat for 30 seconds while the finches are out feeding. (*Note*: Students representing goats are wearing blindfolds not because goats are blind, but because they move through the finches' ecosystem blindly, without paying attention to the birds' nesting sites.) If the goat steps on a paper plate, that nest is destroyed and should be removed from the circle. If the goat encounters a chair, that tree is damaged and should be removed. If the goat touches a bird, that bird is trampled (but birds can fly away from the blindfolded goat). After 30 seconds sound the whistle and have students try to return to a nest. Any birds that do not find a nest site or were trampled must leave the finch population of the circle.

4. For the next round, appoint one of the homeless finches to be a second goat. Repeat the above steps. In each subsequent round, double the number of goats. When all the vegetation is removed, the simulation is over.

Discuss the damage done by the goats to the vegetation and how this damage affects the finch populations.

Were any birds destroyed directly?
Young chicks in ground finch nests might be trampled, but the most damage goats cause is not from harming the birds directly.

How did the goats affect the finches indirectly?
Goats destroyed nests and nesting sites.

Standards

The material promoted in this activity enhances and supports student understanding of the following *National Science Education Standards* for grades 5–8:

Populations and Ecosystems (Life Science)

A population consists of all individuals of a species that occur together at a given place and time. All populations living together and the physical factors with which they interact compose an ecosystem.

Populations of organisms can be categorized by the function they serve in an ecosystem. Plants and some microorganisms are producers—they make their own food. All animals, including humans, are consumers, which obtain food by eating other organisms. Decomposers, primarily bacteria and fungi, are consumers that use waste materials and dead organisms for food. Food webs identify the relationships among producers, consumers, and decomposers in an ecosystem.

The number of organisms an ecosystem can support depends on the resources available and abiotic factors, such as quantity of light and water, range of temperatures, and soil composition. Given adequate biotic and abiotic resources and no disease or predators, populations (including humans) increase at rapid rates. Lack of resources and other factors, such as predation and climate, limit the growth of populations in specific niches in the ecosystem.

Diversity and Adaptations of Organisms (Life Science)

Extinction of a species occurs when the environment changes and the adaptive characteristics of a species are insufficient to allow its survival. Fossils indicate that many organisms that lived long ago are extinct. Extinction of species is common; most of the species that have lived on the Earth no longer exist.

TEACHER SECTION

Assessment

Activity	Exemplary	Emergent	Deficient
Part A	Students are able to develop accurate food webs for the tortoises before and after the introduction of goats on Isabela. They are able to show the relationship of goats to tortoises by creating a concept web or some other illustration.	Students are able to develop a food web of the tortoises before and after the introduction of goats on Isabela only after some teacher coaching. They need help using the concept of a food web to show the relationship of goats to tortoises.	Students have great difficulty developing both a food web and a concept map. They do not understand the concept of introduced or invasive species.
Part B	Students participate in the introduced species simulation and are able to discuss correctly the consequences of invasive goats on Isabela.	Students participate in the introduced species simulation, but do not easily discuss the consequences of the introduced goats.	Students have trouble with the introduced species simulation. They do not understand how introduced goats affect the finch habitat on Isabela.

INTRODUCED GOATS VS. GIANT TORTOISES

The following is a journal entry from Dr. Betsy Jackson, an ecologist doing research on the habitat of the Galápagos giant tortoise, *Geochelone elephantopus*. Dr. Jackson has recently finished her observations of the tortoises of Española Island and has now set up an observation post on the largest island in the Galápagos Archipelago, Isabela. Dr. Jackson is attempting to document the impact of introduced species such as goats on native populations of giant tortoises.

Isabela Island, August 3, 1999

I have finally finished my first round of research in the Galápagos Islands, spending two weeks on Española Island in the southern portion of the Galápagos. I really love Española because of the great variety of animals I was able to observe there. The antics of the sea lions down on the beach and the courting behaviors of the blue-footed and the masked boobies were a delight to watch. Of course, I was really interested in the tortoises, which have been reestablished on the island of Española. While the population numbers are still fairly low, with careful management and protection these wonderful animals should survive.

Now I've begun the next part of my research on Isabela, the biggest island in the Galápagos. The population of tortoises on Isabela is much larger than on Española, but there is a much larger threat to their success—aliens!! These aliens have horns on their head, cloven feet, and eat just about anything. They're not from outer space, though; these aliens are goats. Goats are considered alien to the Galápagos Islands because they were brought to the islands by humans, not nature.

Goats were brought to the islands nearly 200 years ago, and a recent population estimate of goats on Isabela indicates approximately 100,000 animals. The sheer number of goats is the main problem for the tortoises because they compete for the same food. Not only do goats eat plants, they eat all of

INTRODUCED GOATS VS. GIANT TORTOISES

the plants that the tortoises eat. And goats are very good eaters—they eat the native grasses and other vegetation down to the roots—so there is less food for the tortoises, and the plants can hardly recover from the goat grazing activity. Besides being major competitors of the tortoise, these alien goats also affect other animals on Isabela. One of the worst problems is the destruction of ground finch nests. As I walk around the island, I notice areas that show many trampled bird nests, although I never actually saw any goats stepping on them.

The campaign to rid other islands of these competitors to the native tortoise has been pretty successful in the past—goats have been eliminated from Española, Plaza Sur, Santa Fé, Marchena, and Rabida Islands. But Isabela is different. Because it is almost 20 times the size of all these other islands combined, the efforts by the scientists from the Darwin Research Station to eliminate the goats has had little effect on the goat population there.

I have been watching the feeding grounds of the Isabela tortoises for a few days now, and the competition for food does seem to be a problem. Goats eat plants as soon as they start to grow, and the goats are able to migrate from one area to another area on the island fairly easily. Because the tortoises cannot move as quickly or easily over different types of ground, they are not able to move to areas where there may be more food. The recent El Niño of 1997–98 will give some relief because the extra rain will cause the plants to grow more quickly, but I think this is only temporary relief. By the next dry spell, the problem of goat competition will quickly worsen.

I love to watch the tortoises move and graze. There are certainly more of them on Isabela than on Española, but the increased competition for food will be a very big problem unless something is done about the goats.

EVOLUTION
CHAPTER 3

EVOLUTION OF EVOLUTIONARY THOUGHT

Background Information

Although perhaps the most famous, Charles Darwin was not the first great thinker to consider the origin of plants or animals. The question of where life came from had been a topic of discussion for many centuries before Darwin boarded the *Beagle* or wrote *Origin Of Species*. The ancient Greeks speculated about the origins of life and changes in species over time. More than 2,500 years ago, the Greek philosopher Anaximander wrote his theory that a gradual evolution had created the world's living organisms from nonliving material such as dirt, stones, and water.

Leonardo da Vinci, the great scientist and artist, described the shells that were found at the tops of mountains as remains of once-living ocean organisms. His descriptions were precursors to our modern geologic law of superposition. Even Charles Darwin's grandfather, Erasmus Darwin, wrote on the subject. He believed that the process of evolution was the result of organisms being able to acquire new parts as necessary in order to improve themselves and to pass these improvements on down through the generations.

This activity requires good reading comprehension. You may wish to match your students such that different skill levels are represented in each group. Encourage your students to create a glossary for difficult words as they read.

Procedure

This activity introduces students to a number of famous thinkers and scientists from history who pondered the subject of evolution, even long before it was given that name. Distribute the writing selections from Jean-Baptist Lamarck, Charles Darwin, and Alfred Russel Wallace, three scientists who contributed greatly to the ideas behind evolution and natural selection. Divide your class into groups of six and have two students in each group read each selection and discuss its meaning. The questions will be answered by each pair and shared with the rest of the group. To answer all

Objectives

- To investigate the contributions of key scientists in the development of modern evolutionary thought.

- To understand that the concept of evolution is not the contribution of just one person, but is part of a long progression of scientific and philosophical thought predating modern times.

- To learn how to interpret original science writings and how to compare the writings of one scientist to another.

- To understand that many individuals contribute to the traditions of science.

Materials

- Student handouts:

    Thinking About Evolutionary Thought

    Jean-Baptiste Lamarck

    Charles Darwin

    Alfred Russel Wallace

ACTIVITY 15: EVOLUTION OF EVOLUTIONARY THOUGHT

TEACHER SECTION

the questions the students will have to collaborate with one another. The deciphering of the language is instructive, and students should be encouraged to learn from each other. As the groups answer the questions, the teacher should be circulating among the groups to "side coach" their progress. The goal of these questions is to encourage students to read carefully and to think critically about the information presented.

A list of important scientists who have contributed to the development of evolution concepts is provided. As an option, students can use the Internet to investigate the scientists. If enough students participate, you can create a timeline of evolutionary thought from the ancient Greeks up to modern scientists. A sample timeline and excellent Internet resources for this activity can be found at the University of California Museum of Paleontology, Berkeley, http://www.ucmp.berkeley.edu/history/evolution.html.

Influential contributors to evolutionary concepts:

Aristotle (384–322 B.C.E.)

Leonardo da Vinci (1452–1519)

John Ray (1628–1705)

Antony van Leeuwenhoek (1632–1723)

Robert Hooke (1635–1703)

Georges–Louis Leclerc, Comte de Buffon (1707–1788)

Carolus Linnaeus (1707–1778)

Erasmus Darwin (1731–1802)

William Paley (1743–1805)

Jean-Baptiste Lamarck (1744–1829)

Thomas Malthus (1766–1834)

Georges Cuvier (1769–1832)

William Smith (1769–1839)

Étienne Geoffroy St. Hilaire (1772–1844)

Adam Sedgwick (1785–1873)

Patrick Matthew (1790–1874)

Mary Anning (1799–1847)

Sir Richard Owen (1804–1892)

Louis Agassiz (1807–1873)

Charles Darwin (1809–1882)

Gregor Mendel (1822–1884)

Alfred Russel Wallace (1823–1913)

Thomas Henry Huxley (1824–1895)

Ernst Haeckel (1834–1919)

Edward Drinker Cope (1840–1897)

Henry Fairfield Osborn (1857–1935)

Alfred Wegener (1880–1930)

J.B.S. Haldane (1892–1964)

Theodosius Dobzhansky (1900–1975)

Ernst Mayr (1904 –)

Steven J. Gould (1941–)

ACTIVITY 15: EVOLUTION OF EVOLUTIONARY THOUGHT

Answers to student questions:

TEACHER SECTION

1. *How did Lamarck think the environment influences the way organisms evolved?*

    The environment affects the shape and organization of animals, and when the environment changes, it produces corresponding changes in animals. If a new environment causes new behavior, the result will be the use of one part of the body in preference to another, and in some cases the total disuse of some part that is no longer necessary.

2. *What did Lamarck mean by the disuse and use of organs?*

    Parts or organs of animals that are used will become more developed over the life of the animal, and parts or organs that are not used will eventually disappear.

3. *How did Lamarck think new characteristics were obtained by animals?*

    Offspring will inherit only the parts "used" by its parents. If an organism uses and develops a body part it will pass this enhanced part to its offspring— "inheritance of acquired characteristics."

4. *Did Lamarck give an explanation of how organisms changed over a period of time?*

    Yes, Lamarck said organisms changed because of "use and disuse" and then "inheritance of acquired characteristics."

5. *What did Wallace mean by his statement, "The life of wild animals is a struggle for existence"?*

    Wallace was saying that wild animals are constantly vying with each other for survival.

6. *Wallace said that "useful variations will tend to increase, unuseful or hurtful variations to diminish." How could this happen?*

    This is basically natural selection. Organisms with variations that give them advantages over other organisms in a particular environment will survive and pass these advantages on to their offspring. Variations that are not useful or give a disadvantage to an organism are less likely to be passed on because the organism is less likely to survive and therefore not pass on the variations.

ACTIVITY 15: EVOLUTION OF EVOLUTIONARY THOUGHT

TEACHER SECTION

7. *What evidence or example does Wallace give?*

Wallace pointed out that even color change can make an individual more or less noticeable. That change can mean the individual will be either more or less safe from enemies. Major changes can influence how the animal is able to obtain food—a key to survival.

8. *How does Wallace's explanation differ from Lamarck's?*

Wallace explained that variation is normal, and organisms are born with variations, some of which provide survival advantages. Lamarck said the environment caused the changes.

9. *How did Darwin come up with his ideas about the origin of species?*

Darwin came up with his ideas by observing variations in organisms. Based on his observations, he wondered about the origin of different plants and animals and the variations in species he recorded. Some of his observations were made during his five-year voyage around the world on the HMS *Beagle*, but he continued to study natural selection of organisms throughout his life.

10. *What did Darwin say was the cause of the origin of new species?*

Natural selection. That is, organisms vary and some variations give survival advantage. There is a constant struggle for survival, and organisms that survive pass these advantageous variations on to their offspring.

11. *Which paper was easiest to read and understand, Lamarck's, Darwin's, or Wallace's? Why?*

This is open to the student's opinion, although most find Wallace's paper easiest to read and understand because the language is not as difficult.

Standards

The material promoted in this activity enhances and supports student understanding of the following *National Science Education Standards* for grades 5–8:

Diversity and Adaptations of Organisms (Life Science)

Millions of species of animals, plants, and microorganisms are alive today. Although different species might look dissimilar, the unity among organisms becomes apparent from an analysis of internal structures, the similarity of their chemical processes, and the evidence of common ancestry.

Biological evolution accounts for the diversity of species developed through gradual processes over many generations. Species acquire many of their unique characteristics through biological adaptation, which involves the selection of naturally occurring variations in populations. Biological adaptations include changes in structures, behaviors, or physiology that enhance survival and reproductive success in a particular environment.

History of Science (History and Nature of Science)

Many individuals have contributed to the traditions of science. Studying some of these individuals provides further understanding of scientific inquiry, science as a human endeavor, the nature of science, and the relationships between science and society.

In historical perspective, science has been practiced by different individuals in different cultures. In looking at the history of many peoples, one finds that scientists and engineers of high achievement are considered to be among the most valued contributors to their culture.

Tracing the history of science can show how difficult it was for scientific innovators to break through the accepted ideas of their time to reach the conclusions that we currently take for granted.

TEACHER SECTION

Assessment

Activity	Exemplary	Emergent	Deficient
Part A	Students are able to interpret the assigned reading selection. They are able to explain the main points of the historical selection to the other students in their group. The students can answer all the provided questions with little coaching from the teacher.	Students are able to interpret the assigned reading selection with some help from other members of the group and from the teacher. They can only explain the main points of the historical selection with teacher coaching. The students can answer most of the provided questions.	Students have great difficulty interpreting the assigned selections or cannot understand them at all. Teacher coaching is required for all questions. Students cannot help others in their group.
Part B	Students are able to construct a complete timeline of evolutionary concepts after receiving the list of famous contributors.	Students can make a partial timeline of evolutionary thought, but some contributors are missing.	Students have a great deal of difficulty placing the famous scientists correctly on a timeline or need a great deal of teacher coaching to create a timeline.

THINKING ABOUT EVOLUTIONARY THOUGHT

Your teacher will give you one or more handouts of scientific writings by people who are famous for their work on the theory of evolution. To answer the questions below you will need to read your selection very carefully and refer back to the handout. Answer these questions on a separate sheet of paper.

1. How did Lamark think the environment influences the way organisms evolved?

2. What did Lamarck mean by the disuse and use of organs?

3. How did Lamarck think new characteristics were obtained by animals?

4. Did Lamarck give an explanation of how organisms changed over a period of time?

5. What did Wallace mean by his statement, "The life of wild animals is a struggle for existence"?

6. Wallace said that "useful variations will tend to increase, unuseful or hurtful variations to diminish." How could this happen?

7. What evidence or example does Wallace give?

8. How does Wallace's explanation differ from Lamarck's?

9. How did Darwin come up with his ideas about the origin of species?

10. What did Darwin say was the cause of the origin of new species?

11. Which paper was easiest to read and understand, Lamarck's, Darwin's, or Wallace's? Why?

JEAN-BAPTISTE LAMARCK (1744–1829)

PHILOSOPHIE ZOOLOGIQUE, 1809

(Translated by H. Elliott, Macmillan Company, London. 1914.)

The environment affects the shape and organization of animals; that is to say that when the environment becomes very different, it produces in course of time corresponding modifications in the shape and organization of animals.

If a new environment, which has become permanent for some race of animals, induces new habits in these animals, that is to say, leads them into new activities which become habitual, the result will be the use of some one part in preference to some other part, and in some cases the total disuse of some part no longer necessary.

Nothing of all this can be considered as hypothesis or private opinion; on the contrary, they are truths which, in order to be made clear, only require attention and the observation of facts.

Snakes have adopted the habit of crawling on the ground and hiding in the grass; so that their body, as a result of continually repeated efforts at elongation for the purpose of passing through narrow spaces, has acquired a considerable length, quite out of proportion to its size. Now, legs would have been quite useless to these animals and consequently unused. Long legs would have interfered with their need of crawling, and very short legs would have been incapable of moving their body, since they could only have had four. The disuse of these parts thus

JEAN-BAPTISTE LAMARCK

became permanent in the various races of these animals, and resulted in the complete disappearance of these same parts, although legs really belong to the plan or organization of the animals of this class.

The frequent use of any organ, when confirmed by habit, increases the functions of that organ, leads to its development, and endows it with a size and power that it does not possess in animals which exercise it less.

We have seen that the disuse of any organ modifies, reduces, and finally extinguishes it. I shall now prove that the constant use of any organ, accompanied by efforts to get the most out of it, strengthens and enlarges that organ, or creates new ones to carry on the functions that have become necessary.

The bird which is drawn to the water by its need of finding there the prey on which it lives, separates the digits of its feet in trying to strike the water and move about on the surface. The skin which unites these digits at their base acquires the habit of being stretched by these continually repeated separations of the digits; thus in course of time there are formed large webs which unite the digits of ducks, geese, etc. as we actually find them.

It is interesting to observe the result of habit in the peculiar shape and size of the giraffe; this animal, the largest of the mammals, is known to live in the interior of Africa in places where the soil is nearly always arid and barren, so that it is obliged to browse on the leaves of trees and to make constant efforts to reach them. From this habit long maintained in all its race, it has resulted that the animal's fore-legs have become longer than its hind legs, and that its neck is lengthened to such a degree that the giraffe, without standing up on its hind legs, attains a height of six meters.

CHARLES DARWIN (1809–1882)

ON THE ORIGIN OF SPECIES, 1859

When on board HMS *Beagle*, as naturalist, I was much struck with certain facts in the distribution of the inhabitants of South America, and in the geological relations of the present to the past inhabitants of that continent. These facts seemed to me to throw some light on the origin of species—that mystery of mysteries, as it has been called by one of our greatest philosophers. On my return home, it occurred to me, in 1837, that something might perhaps be made out of this question by patiently accumulating and reflecting on all sorts of facts which could possibly have any bearing on it.

My work is now nearly finished; but as it will take me two or three more years to complete it, and as my health is far from strong, I have been urged to publish this Abstract. I have more especially been induced to do this, as Mr. Wallace, who is now studying the natural history of the Malay Archipelago, has arrived at almost exactly the same general conclusions that I have on the origin of species. Last year he sent to me a memoir on this subject.

In considering the origin of species, it is quite conceivable that a naturalist, reflecting on the mutual affinities of organic beings, on their embryological relations, their geographical distribution, geological succession, and other such facts, might come to the conclusion that each species had not been independently created, but had descended, like varieties, from other species. Nevertheless, such a conclusion, even if well founded, would be unsatisfactory, until it could be shown how the innumerable species inhabiting this world have been modified, so as to acquire that perfection of structure and coadaptation which most justly excites our admiration. Naturalists continually refer to external conditions, such as climate, food, etc., as the only possible cause of variation. In one very

ACTIVITY 15: EVOLUTION OF EVOLUTIONARY THOUGHT

CHARLES DARWIN

limited sense, as we shall hereafter see, this may be true; but it is preposterous to attribute to mere external conditions, the structure, for instance, of the woodpecker, with its feet, tail, beak, and tongue, so admirable adapted to catch insects under the bark of trees.

No one ought to feel surprise at much remaining as yet unexplained in regard to the origin of species and varieties, if he makes due allowance for our profound ignorance in regard to the mutual relations of all the beings which live around us. Who can explain why one species ranges widely and is very numerous, and why another allied species has a narrow range and is rare? Yet these relations are of the highest importance, for they determine the present welfare, and, as I believe, the future success and modification of every inhabitant of this world. Still less do we know of the mutual relations of the innumerable inhabitants of the world during the many past geological epochs in its history. Although much remains obscure, and will long remain obscure, I can entertain no doubt, after the most deliberate study and dispassionate judgment of which I am capable, that the view which most naturalists entertain, and which I formerly entertained—namely, that each species has been independently created—is erroneous. I am fully convinced that species are not immutable; but that those belonging to what are called the same genera are lineal descendants of some other and generally extinct species, in the same manner as the acknowledged varieties of any one species are the descendants of that species. Furthermore, I am convinced that Natural Selection has been the main but not exclusive means of modification.

ALFRED RUSSEL WALLACE (1823–1913)

ON THE TENDENCY OF VARIETIES TO DEPART INDEFINITELY FROM THE ORIGINAL TYPE, 1858

The Struggle for Existence

The life of wild animals is a struggle for existence. The full exertion of all their faculties and all their energies is required to preserve their own existence and provide for that of their infant offspring. The possibility of procuring food during the least favorable seasons and of escaping the attacks of their most dangerous enemies are the primary conditions which determine the existence both of individuals and of entire species. The numbers that die annually must be immense; and as the individual existence of each animal depends upon itself, those that die must be the weakest—the very young, the aged, and the diseased—while those that prolong their existence can only be the most perfect in health and vigor, those who are best able to obtain food regularly and avoid their numerous enemies. It is "a struggle for existence," in which the weakest and least perfectly organized must always succumb.

Useful Variations will Tend to Increase, Unuseful or Hurtful Variations to Diminish

Most or perhaps all the variations from the typical form of a species must have some definite effect, however slight, on the habits or capacities of the individuals. Even a change of color might, by rendering them more or less distinguishable, affect their safety; a

ALFRED RUSSEL WALLACE

greater or lesser development of hair might modify their habits. More important changes, such as an increase in the power or dimensions of the limbs or any of the external organs, would more or less affect their mode of procuring food or the range of country which they could inhabit. It is also evident that most changes would affect, either favorably or adversely, the powers of prolonging existence. An antelope with shorter or weaker legs must necessarily suffer more from the attacks of the feline carnivora; the passenger pigeon with less powerful wings would sooner or later be affected in its powers of procuring a regular supply of food; and in both cases the result must necessarily be a diminution of the population of the modified species. If, on the other hand, any species should produce a variety having slightly increased powers of preserving existence, that variety must inevitably in time acquire a superiority in numbers.

SIMILAR BUT DIFFERENT:
THE KEY TO CLASSIFICATION

Background Information

Classification of organisms is an important process for field biologists. Classification includes the investigation of genetic relationships among organisms and their placement into an organized system. The modern approach to biological classification was largely founded by the Swedish naturalist Carolus Linnaeus in the eighteenth century. His system for naming, ranking, and classifying organisms is still used widely today, although it has been modified somewhat from his original plan.

Charles Darwin spent most of his life doing research that involved the classification of plants and animals. Even as a young man he collected and classified all kinds of insects, especially beetles. During his 1835 exploration of the Galápagos, Darwin noted the variety of life forms that existed throughout the archipelago:

> ...by far the most remarkable feature in the natural history of this archipelago... is that the different islands to a considerable extent are inhabited by a different set of beings. My attention was first called to this fact by the Vice-Governor, Mr. Lawson, declaring that the tortoises differed from the different islands, and that he could with certainty tell from which island any one was brought.

This activity will introduce the concept of *classification*, *taxonomy*, *dichotomous keys*, and grouping in a fun way. Students will become familiar with the process of classification and learn how to make a classification key. Then they will classify some of the reptiles Darwin saw when he visited the Galápagos.

Taxonomy is the branch of study that deals with the classification of organisms. Taxonomists use dichotomous keys prepared by scientists who are experts on a particular group. The purpose of these keys is to make classification of that group easier for other, non-experts, by giving them a structured pattern to follow.

TEACHER SECTION
This activity is modified from a version created by NSTA for the Smithsonian Institution for the film *Galapagos in 3D*. An online adaptation of this activity can be found at http://pubs.nsta.org/galapagos/.

Objectives

- To investigate the uses of classification in science research.

- To learn how to construct a dichotomous key for a variety of organisms or objects.

- To classify Galápagos reptiles based on descriptions and illustrations.

Materials

- Student handout:

    Galápagos Reptiles

- Paper

- Pens or pencils

- Field guides to local or other habitats (optional)

TEACHER SECTION

People can use dichotomous keys to classify almost anything—animals, plants, minerals, bacteria, etc.—into specific categories. The structure of a dichotomous key is built by dividing a group of objects into two categories based on a particular characteristic. Each category is then subdivided by different criteria until each group has only one example. It is called a dichotomous key because each group is divided into two subgroups each time.

You can tie this activity into students' study of their local environment or another habitat. Students can look through field guides of the area and create dichotomous keys for the organisms listed.

Procedure

Part A

In Part A, students learn how to use and design a simple dichotomous key by using the population of shoes in their own classroom. They will construct a "Class Classification" key by picking a characteristic that will divide the whole group of shoes into two groups.

Before they begin, introduce the concepts of classification, taxonomy, and dichotomous keys. Then have the students remove their shoes, putting all the left shoes into one pile and the right shoes into another. Divide the class into two groups, each working with one pile. You may want to separate the piles into opposite ends of the classroom so the groups will work independently. Ask the students to think of classifying questions and then physically form groups according to the results. Assign one student to record each group's set of questions. All the questions need to have "yes or no" answers. For example, "does the shoe have laces?" will divide the shoes into two subgroups: those with laces such as athletic shoes and hiking boots vs. slip-on shoes and shoes with velcro.

The next question might be "of the shoes with laces, is the shoe black?" This will divide the shoes into two smaller groups: black shoes with laces, and shoes with laces that are any color other than black. Note the question is not "what color is the shoe?" because that would lead to more than two possible groupings (black, brown, white, blue, etc.). Only the two groups "black" and "not black" make a dichotomy.

Continue these questions until every unique shoe has its own category. You have now designed a key that will define each shoe in your class (e.g., one shoe ends up being defined as a laced, black, heeled, suede boot). If more than one student wears the exact same shoe in the same size, both shoes may end up in the same category, just as two organisms of the same species would be in the same category.

After both teams are done, write their questions on the board and compare their results. Other items can also be classified as practice or extension exercises, such as different types of kitchen tools, pasta, or even laboratory glassware. Students can even do homework classifying anything from music collections to stuffed animals.

Part B

Part B of the activity will help your students apply what they have learned about classification and dichotomous keys. They will design a key to classify the reptiles of the Galápagos Islands using drawings and descriptions.

Divide your class into groups of three or four and distribute copies of the student handout *Galápagos Reptiles*. Students should put their classifying questions on a separate sheet of paper. After they have completed the exercise, groups will switch papers to test each others' keys by trying to classify the animals according to the criteria decided upon by the other group.

To divide a group of organisms into two categories, students can begin with a question such as "Does the animal have legs?" Animals that do have legs would then be classified in one group, and animals with no legs would be classified into a second group. Below is a sample answer key, but of course there can be any number of "correct" keys. The most important part of this activity is learning how to observe the many variations of organisms that have evolved throughout the archipelago.

TEACHER SECTION

Sample dichotomous key:

1A	Legs present	Go to number 2
1B	Legs absent	Galápagos snake
2A	Shell present	Go to number 3
2B	Shell absent	Go to number 5
3A	Legs not flipper-like	Go to number 4
3B	Legs flipper-like	Green sea turtle
4A	Shell is shaped like a dome, with the front opening not highly arched	Dome-shaped giant tortoise
4B	Shell is saddle-shaped, with the front opening highly arched	Saddleback giant tortoise
5A	Adult animal longer than 50 cm from nose to tip of tail; distinct spines on back	Go to number 6
5B	Adult animal less than 50 cm (usually 15–25 cm) from nose to tip of tail; no or very small spines on back	Lava lizard
6A	Body color mostly black, tail somewhat compressed (flattened), snout (nose) flat, behavior includes swimming in ocean	Marine iguana
6B	Body color mostly tan, yellow on top, darker below; tail not compressed; inhabits land	Land iguana

Standards

The material promoted in this activity enhances and supports student understanding of the following *National Science Education Standards* for grades 5–8:

Understandings about Scientific Inquiry (Science as Inquiry)

Different kinds of questions suggest different kinds of scientific investigations. Some investigations involve observing and describing objects, organisms, or events; some involve collecting specimens; some involve experiments; some involve seeking more information; some involve discovery of new objects and phenomena; and some involve making models.

Reproduction and Heredity (Life Science)

The characteristics of an organism can be described in terms of a combination of traits. Some traits are inherited and others result from interactions with the environment.

Diversity and Adaptations of Organisms (Life Science)

Millions of species of animals, plants, and microorganisms are alive today. Although different species might look dissimilar, the unity among organisms becomes apparent from an analysis of internal structures, the similarity of their chemical processes, and the evidence of common ancestry.

Assessment

Activity	Exemplary	Emergent	Deficient
Part A	Students work well in a group and are able to use and design a simple dichotomous key by using the population of their shoes, with little teacher coaching.	Students work moderately well in a group and are able to use and design a simple dichotomous key of their shoes, with some teacher coaching.	Students are not able to use and design a simple dichotomous key even with teacher coaching.
Part B	Students are able to design a dichotomous key of Galápagos reptiles from the descriptions and drawings provided, with little teacher coaching.	Students are able to design a dichotomous key of Galápagos reptiles from the descriptions and drawings provided, with some teacher coaching.	Students are not able to design a dichotomous key of Galápagos reptiles from the descriptions and drawings provided.

GALÁPAGOS REPTILES

When Charles Darwin visited the coast of South America and the Galápagos Islands, he was interested in finding as many plants and animals as possible. Years later, as he was writing his books, he reflected on the many varieties of animals he collected and identified. Reptiles were some of the most incredible animals Darwin saw on the islands. This activity will help you to classify many of those same reptiles. Using the descriptions and drawings of nine of the reptiles that live in the Galápagos, you will construct a dichotomous classification key for these animals. Put your questions on one sheet of paper and your answers on another, so that other groups can test your key.

Be sure to make your questions as clear as possible, because later scientists and explorers will need to use the key to identify the reptiles they encounter as they search the Galápagos habitats.

Remember, to make a dichotomous key you will divide entire groups of reptiles into two groups based on some characteristic. Then each subgroup will be further divided into groups of two until each group contains only one species.

When you have finished, trade keys with another group, so you can test each others' results.

Green sea turtles are much smaller than the giant tortoises, ranging from 50 to 100 kg (occasionally up to 150 kg). These marine turtles have flipper-like legs that enable them to swim for thousands of kilometers in the seas around the Galápagos, feeding mostly on ulva (a seaweed-like algae), jellyfish, and crustaceans.

The **marine iguana** is the only sea-going lizard in the world and is found exclusively in the Galápagos Islands, inhabiting many of the coastal stretches. Marine iguanas range from 25 to 60 cm and are mainly black with some slight variations of red and green. They have short snouts (noses), spiny crowns along the head and back, and flat tails that they use as they swim in the sea. These iguanas feed on algae and seaweed and can dive down to 12 m in search of food.

GALÁPAGOS REPTILES

There are three varieties of **Galápagos snakes**, all of which are constrictor-type snakes that grow up to 1 m long. Their diet consists mainly of small reptiles, insects, and bird hatchlings.

Lava lizards are small and multi-colored, growing up to 30 cm long. They are found on many of the Galápagos Islands, especially in the arid lowlands. These lizards feed mostly on moths, grasshoppers, beetles, and other insects. Their coloration often matches the kind of environments in which they live—those living on islands with black lava tend to be darker than those living on sandy beaches.

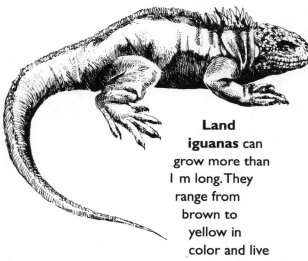

Land iguanas can grow more than 1 m long. They range from brown to yellow in color and live inland on several islands. Land iguana tails are rounder than those of the marine iguana, their noses are longer, and they do not have as pronounced a spiny back as their seagoing relatives. Land iguanas feed mostly on the flowers and pads of the prickly-pear cactus.

Giant tortoises are extremely large land-dwelling reptiles, weighing up to 270 kg. Tortoises on the Galápagos can be divided into two major groups: smaller **saddleback tortoises** and larger **dome-shaped tortoises**. The saddleback tortoises are found in arid zones that have less vegetation for them to feed upon. The raised front of the carapace (shell) allows saddleback tortoises to reach greater heights to eat food such as cactus pads that might otherwise be out of reach. Dome-shaped tortoises live on islands with lush, low-lying vegetation, such as grasses and shrubs.

ISOLATION AND ADAPTATION:
IS SURVIVAL IN THE CARDS?

Background Information

This activity is a highly simplified model of the evolutionary process as it may occur in an archipelago such as the Galápagos. This game demonstrates how, through natural selection and random events, different bird species might evolve on an island archipelago. Ask your students if any of them look exactly like either of their parents. Explain that no one does, because all the characteristics that make up an organism are subject to change from one generation to the next.

A later activity, *Natural Selection: Battle of the Bird Beaks*, will delve more deeply into the idea of natural selection, but you can review the basics here. Stress that most evolutionary changes neither harm nor help the organism's chance of survival.

One example of this neutral type of adaptation in animals is the number of spots on a frog's side. Having three spots is neither more nor less beneficial to a frog's survival than having six spots.

Occasionally, though, changes occur that will harm an organism's chance of survival. For example, a frog may be born without webbing between its toes. Because it would not be able to swim as well as other frogs, it would be less likely to survive and reproduce offspring that may also have this trait.

Just as infrequently, changes occur that enhance an organism's chance of survival, such as the ability to use a food source that others of its kind cannot use. One example might be the hatching of a frog whose tongue is longer than the tongues of other frogs. This frog might be able to catch flies other frogs couldn't reach. Its chance of surviving and passing on this beneficial trait to its offspring would be enhanced. If this group of frogs should become isolated from other frogs—perhaps on an island—over thousands of years, other changes might occur to make these frogs so different from their original group that they would form a separate species.

Objectives

• To model the evolution of different bird species from a common ancestor.

• To observe how certain variations of a species might have an increased chance of survival through natural selection.

• To discuss the random nature of species evolution.

Materials

• Student handouts:

　Set-Up Instructions

　Playing Instructions

　Playing Board (best if copied onto a heavy, white card stock)

　Event Cards (two copies per group, cut along the dotted lines; best if copied onto colored card stock)

　Bird Cards (two copies per group, cut along the dotted lines; best if copied onto different colored card stock than the *Event Cards*)

　Data Sheet

• One six-sided die for each student team

• Transparent tape

• Pencils

• Scissors

TEACHER SECTION

Topic: adaptation

Go to: www.scilinks.org

Code: EE178A

Topic: natural selection

Go to: www.scilinks.org

Code: EE178B

Topic: evolution

Go to: www.scilinks.org

Code: EE178C

Random events might enhance or diminish the survival chances of these new, longer-tongued frogs. If a long-tongued frog should find itself on an island in the middle of a lake with plenty of high-flying flies, future generations of this frog will flourish. If, however, it swims to an island with no flies, and it has no ability to use other food sources, the frog and its descendants will not survive.

Procedure

1. Before class, copy the student handouts *Playing Board, Event Cards,* and *Bird Cards* onto card stock paper if possible. The other handouts, *Set-Up Instructions, Playing Instructions,* and *Data Sheet,* can be on regular paper. The two halves of the *Playing Board* should be taped together. Two copies each of the *Event Cards* and *Bird Cards,* cut along the dotted lines, should be enough for each group. (Depending on the students skill level, they may be able to do the cutting and taping.)

2. Divide the class into groups of three to four. Supply each group with the *Playing Board,* cut-up *Event Cards* and *Bird Cards,* and one copy of the *Set-Up Instructions, Playing Instructions,* and *Data Sheet.*

3. Explain to the students that each event in this activity represents a period of approximately 10,000 years. Events are of two kinds:

    • Adaptation. If an adaptation card is drawn from the pile, assume that over a period of time enough changes have occurred in a population of birds—including changes in beak structure that allow the bird to take advantage of a different food supply—that it has become a different species. These changes can happen only if food the bird can eat is available on the island. If that food is not available, assume that the birds with the new beak structure could not compete successfully for food and did not survive to form a new species. (This is a simplification, and students may ask how a bird would adapt to eat a food that is not on the island. Assume that type of food had been available at one time and has since been wiped out by changing environmental conditions.)

    • Migration. The islands in the Galápagos Archipelago are so far apart that most birds don't normally migrate between them. However, if a migration card is drawn from the pile, assume that several birds of one species were blown out to sea in a storm and landed on a different island. In order for this population of birds to become established on the island, its food source must be available. If the food is not available, the birds will be unable to colonize the new island.

4. Set the scene by explaining that there must be a bird from which the other birds evolve—an ancestral bird. Therefore, the first event of this game occurs before play begins: A group of hard-seed-eating birds, the ancestral species, migrates from the mainland to Island 1 of the archipelago.

5. Let the students read over the instructions before beginning to play.

6. Allow the groups to play for 10 to 15 minutes before they tally their results onto the *Data Sheet*.

After groups tally their results and record them on the *Data Sheet*, invite one student from each group to present the group's results to the class or to write the group's results on the blackboard to show the range of results. Compare and discuss why each group came up with different results. Emphasize the random nature of events, and remind students of the long span of time in which evolutionary events actually occur.

Standards

The material promoted in this activity enhances and supports student understanding of the following *National Science Education Standards* for grades 5–8:

Reproduction and Heredity (Life Science)

In many species, including humans, females produce eggs and males produce sperm. Plants also reproduce sexually—the egg and sperm are produced in the flowers of flowering plants. An egg and sperm unite to begin development of a new individual. That new individual receives genetic information from its mother (via the egg) and its father (via the sperm). Sexually produced offspring never are identical to either of their parents.

Every organism requires a set of instructions for specifying its traits. Heredity is the passage of these instructions from one generation to another.

TEACHER SECTION

The characteristics of an organism can be described in terms of a combination of traits. Some traits are inherited and others result from interactions with the environment.

Populations and Ecosystems (Life Science)

A population consists of all individuals of a species that occur together at a given place and time. All populations living together and the physical factors with which they interact compose an ecosystem.

The number of organisms an ecosystem can support depends on the resources available and abiotic factors, such as quantity of light and water, range of temperatures, and soil composition. Given adequate biotic and abiotic resources and no disease or predators, populations (including humans) increase at rapid rates. Lack of resources and other factors, such as predation and climate, limit the growth of populations in specific niches in the ecosystem.

Diversity and Adaptations of Organisms (Life Science)

Millions of species of animals, plants, and microorganisms are alive today. Although different species might look dissimilar, the unity among organisms becomes apparent from an analysis of internal structures, the similarity of their chemical processes, and the evidence of common ancestry.

Biological evolution accounts for the diversity of species developed through gradual processes over many generations. Species acquire many of their unique characteristics through biological adaptation, which involves the selection of naturally occurring variations in populations. Biological adaptations include changes in structures, behaviors, or physiology that enhance survival and reproductive success in a particular environment.

Extinction of a species occurs when the environment changes and the adaptive characteristics of a species are insufficient to allow its survival. Fossils indicate that many organisms that lived long ago are extinct. Extinction of species is common; most of the species that have lived on the Earth no longer exist.

Assessment

Activity	Exemplary	Emergent	Deficient
	Students correctly follow instructions to play the finch game. They finish the game and give a complete report to the remainder of the class.	Students are able to play the game with some assistance from other groups or from the teacher. They give a report to the class that demonstrates limited understanding of adaptation and survival.	Students do not complete an entire game or have difficulty completing it. They are not able to give a report to the remainder of the class.

SET-UP INSTRUCTIONS

1. Place the two-page playing board on the table and tape the two halves together.

2. Shuffle the *Event Cards* and place them face down in the space on the board labeled "Event Cards."

3. Place the *Bird Card* that says "Ancestral Bird" on Island 1. Note that the food for this bird is available on this island.

4. Separate the remaining *Bird Cards* into six piles by number and place them face up in the labeled spaces on the board.

5. Keep the *Playing Instructions* in a convenient place for reference.

6. Use the chart below to see which finches eat which food type.

Beak and seed key:

Large crushing beak			Hard seeds
Small crushing beak			Soft seeds
Fruit-eating beak			Fleshy fruit
Wood-chiseling beak			Grubs
Tweezer-like beak			Caterpillars
Nectar-sipping beak			Flower nectar

PLAYING INSTRUCTIONS

1. Draw an *Event Card*. Until birds have arrived on other islands, all instructions apply to Island 1. If birds are present on two or more islands, roll the die and apply the *Event Card* to whichever island's number comes up first.

a. If the card is an *Adaptation Card*, consult the beak and seed key to learn what type of food that bird is adapted to eat.

• If the bird's food is available, add the corresponding *Bird Card* to the other cards on the island and discard the used *Event Card*.

• If that *Bird Card* is already on the island, draw again.

• If its food is not available, discard the used *Event Card* and do not move a *Bird Card* to the island.

b. If a *Migration Card* is drawn and more than one type of bird is on the starting island, roll the die and move the bird whose number comes up first. Consult the beak and seed key to learn what type of food that bird is adapted to eat.

• If the bird's food is available on the new island, add a corresponding *Bird Card* to the island and discard the used *Event Card*. If a *Migration Card* names an island where the bird is already located, draw again.

• If its food is not available, discard the used *Event Card* and leave the *Bird Card* on the original island.

2. If the ancestral bird dies for lack of food (it migrates to an island that does not have its food type), begin a new game immediately.

3. When all the event cards have been used once, shuffle the cards and begin again. The activity ends when the teacher calls time.

4. At the end of the last game, record on the *Data Sheet* handout which birds are living on which islands. Prepare your results to present to the rest of the class.

PLAYING BOARD

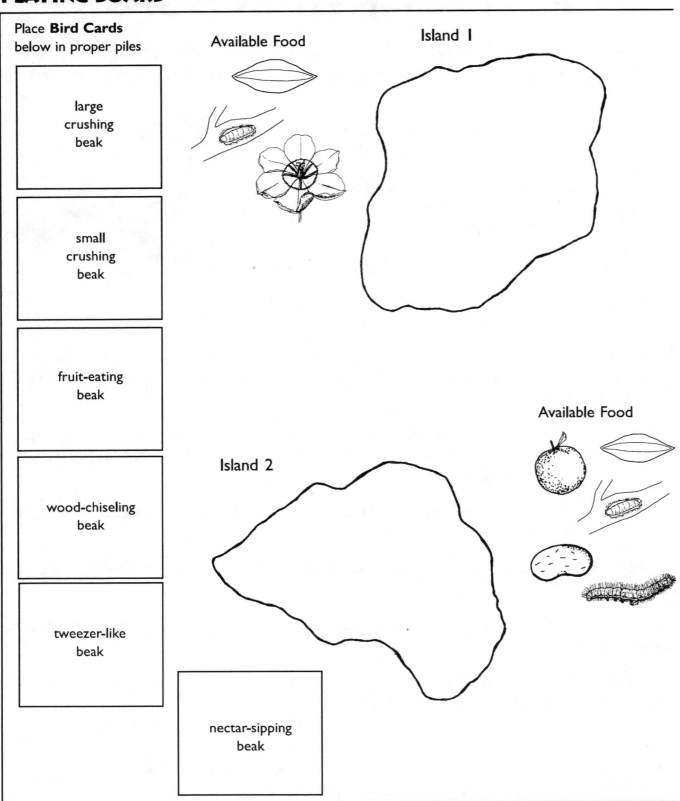

Place **Bird Cards** below in proper piles

large crushing beak

small crushing beak

fruit-eating beak

wood-chiseling beak

tweezer-like beak

nectar-sipping beak

Available Food

Island 1

Island 2

Available Food

PLAYING BOARD

Discarded Bird Cards

Event Cards

Discarded Event Cards

Island 3

Available Food

Available Food

Island 4

Island 5

Available Food

ACTIVITY 17: ISOLATION AND ADAPTATION

EVENT CARDS

Adaptation Card	fruit-eating beak	Adaptation Card	nectar-sipping beak	Migration Card	Migrate to Island 2	Migration Card	Migrate to Island 4	Migration Card	Migrate to Island 5
Adaptation Card	fruit-eating beak	Adaptation Card	nectar-sipping beak	Migration Card	Migrate to Island 2	Migration Card	Migrate to Island 4	Migration Card	Migrate to Island 5
Adaptation Card	small crushing beak	Adaptation Card	tweezer-like beak	Migration Card	Migrate to Island 2	Migration Card	Migrate to Island 4	Migration Card	Migrate to Island 5
Adaptation Card	small crushing beak	Adaptation Card	tweezer-like beak	Migration Card	Migrate to Island 1	Migration Card	Migrate to Island 3	Migration Card	Move half of species to Island 4. Leave bird card behind and move a new one of the same type.
Adaptation Card	large crushing beak	Adaptation Card	wood-chiseling beak	Migration Card	Migrate to Island 1	Migration Card	Migrate to Island 3	Migration Card	Move half of species to Island 2. Leave bird card behind and move a new one of the same type.
Adaptation Card	large crushing beak	Adaptation Card	wood-chiseling beak	Migration Card	Migrate to Island 1	Migration Card	Migrate to Island 3	Ancestral Bird Card	large crushing beak

BIRD CARDS

Bird Card — nectar-sipping beak	Bird Card — nectar-sipping beak	Bird Card — nectar-sipping beak	Bird Card — nectar-sipping beak	Bird Card — nectar-sipping beak
Bird Card — tweezer-like beak	Bird Card — tweezer-like beak	Bird Card — tweezer-like beak	Bird Card — tweezer-like beak	Bird Card — tweezer-like beak
Bird Card — wood-chiseling beak	Bird Card — wood-chiseling beak	Bird Card — wood-chiseling beak	Bird Card — wood-chiseling beak	Bird Card — wood-chiseling beak
Bird Card — fruit-eating beak	Bird Card — fruit-eating beak	Bird Card — fruit-eating beak	Bird Card — fruit-eating beak	Bird Card — fruit-eating beak
Bird Card — small crushing beak	Bird Card — small crushing beak	Bird Card — small crushing beak	Bird Card — small crushing beak	Bird Card — small crushing beak
Bird Card — large crushing beak	Bird Card — large crushing beak	Bird Card — large crushing beak	Bird Card — large crushing beak	Bird Card — large crushing beak

DATA SHEET

List which birds migrated to or evolved on each island:

Island 1: _____

_____

_____

_____

Species surviving at the end of game: _____

Island 2: _____

_____

_____

_____

Species surviving at the end of game: _____

Island 3: _____

_____

_____

_____

Species surviving at the end of game: _____

Island 4: _____

_____

_____

_____

Species surviving at the end of game: _____

Island 5: _____

_____

_____

_____

Species surviving at the end of game: _____

NATURAL SELECTION:

BATTLE OF THE BIRD BEAKS

TEACHER SECTION
This activity is modified from a version created by NSTA for the Smithsonian Institution for the film *Galapagos in 3D*.

Background Information

This activity introduces students to the concepts of natural selection and adaptation. Both of these concepts are integral to understanding the mechanisms of evolution. Darwin's focus on how evolution works centers around the concept of natural selection. Although he did not describe the natural selection of organisms in the Galápagos Islands while he was there in 1835, he certainly reflected on his many observations of Galápagos plants and animals when he wrote his *Journal of Travels On Board the HMS* Beagle and especially when he wrote *Origin of Species* published in 1859.

In addition to discussing the diversity of the giant tortoises on the different islands, Darwin noted the differences in the finches he observed and collected. These 13 species of finches are now collectively called Darwin's Finches. They vary in size and especially in the structure of their beaks. The beaks of these Galápagos finches have been the subject of many books and articles and have studied extensively as models of evolution, adaptation, and natural selection.

As Darwin noted, the concept is often misunderstood: Species don't change in order to survive in a particular environment, they simply change. Each individual is different from other individuals in the species, so within a given population a great deal of normal variation occurs. Almost always, more individuals are born, hatched, germinated, etc. than their environment can maintain. Therefore, some individuals live to maturity and reproduce, and some do not. If an organism is better able to survive because of a variation, then the organism has an advantage. If an organism is more likely to die because of a variation, the trait is disadvantageous. Those with advantageous traits are more likely to survive and possibly pass those traits onto their offspring. If those offspring also have that trait, then they may also be more likely to survive. Of course, what is advantageous during one generation may not be during later generations if the environmental pressures change. Thus, the environment "selects" individuals that are better able to survive. This is natural selection.

Objectives

- To learn the concepts of competition and adaptation as they apply to natural selection.

- To understand that some adaptations will give competitive advantages.

- To understand that the benefits of adaptations can change when environments change.

Materials

- Student handouts:

    Battle of the Bird Beaks

    Data Chart

- "Finch Food":

    Rice grains (white, long grain rice)

    Dried peas (or red beans or similar food)

- Two pieces of patterned cloth or gift wrap paper (.5 m x .5 m). Choose one cloth with a main color that will match the rice (white) and one that will match the peas (green).

- Containers to hold the "finch food"

- Tweezers—either metal or plastic (enough for the entire class)

- Stopwatch

- Whistle or other signaling mechanism

- Graph paper

TEACHER SECTION

A famous, ongoing study of natural selection has been conducted by Peter and Rosemary Grant of Princeton University. For almost 30 years, the Grants have studied populations of Darwin's finches on the small island of Daphne Major, off the coast of Santa Cruz Island. The Grants have studied the changes and adaptations of two species of finch in particular, the medium ground finch and the cactus finch. As noted in the previous activity, a great deal of variation occurs in finches, especially in their size and beak shape.

In this activity, the food units represent two different seed types gathered by the finches on Daphne Major. The peas represent large seeds and the rice represents smaller seeds. The two background colors represent different environmental conditions: an arid zone versus a humid zone that receives a lot of rainfall.

This activity allows the students to plot changes in seed populations along with changes in population size of the different beaked finches on Daphne Major. Of course, the lab activity does not show evolution of an entirely new species in three generations, but it does demonstrate the force of natural selection on populations of birds that show variation in the size of their beaks. Students should be encouraged to graph their results and discuss what the results indicate about natural selection of the birds. They should also discuss natural selection of the finches' food sources, changes in environmental conditions, and the influence of competition in natural selection.

Procedure

Set-Up

Have students count off so that you begin with three or four teams of three students each, with the rest of the students waiting on the sidelines. If your class is very small, you may have to start with just two teams, but three or four is better to allow for variation. Each student on the sideline will then take a number 1, 2, 3, 4, etc. The lowest-numbered person will join the game at the first opportunity. Then the next in line will join, and so on. When a bird "dies" it goes to the sidelines at the end of the line and waits to be "born."

One student on each team should be selected as the team Evolutionary Biologist who manages the finch study and records the results. The other two students will be finches. The finches are of two types—a large-beaked finch and a small-beaked finch. The rest of the students on the sidelines will wait until one finch has been successful in obtaining a certain amount of food and therefore will "produce" an offspring: another finch of the same type. A new student will enter the game as that offspring.

Distribute one type of cloth or paper background for half of the teams and the other color background for the other half. These represent two different environmental conditions on the island of Daphne Major.

Rules

The large-beaked finches will use their fingers as "beaks" to pick up food. They can only pick up food with two fingers by pinching them together to get the small food unit (grain of rice) or the large food unit (dried pea), and they may only pick up one piece of food at a time. The small-beaked finches will use tweezers as beaks. They may also pick up only one piece of food at a time. Once each finch picks up the food, he or she deposits it in a paper cup and gets another piece of food.

To maintain consistency, you should control the "feeding seasons," which last for 20 seconds. Signal the start and end of a feeding season with the whistle. Start the first season with 100 large food units and 200 small food units. Each finch will take a 20-second turn feeding, but he or she can select only one piece of food at a time. *Only one bird feeds at a time.* The finch to the right of the Evolutionary Biologist will go first. (You can modify these rules to allow the birds to feed at the same time, increasing competition, but the results may be messy.) At the end of each feeding season the students will count how many of each food type they selected, and the Evolutionary Biologist will record this number on the *Data Chart* handout.

To survive, a bird must gather a certain number of food units—10 large food units or 20 small food units (or any combination—one large food unit equals two small food units). If it does not gather enough food, the finch "dies" and joins the rest of the students on the sidelines waiting to be "born."

If the finch gets enough food it will not only survive, it will reproduce. Once a finch gathers 20 large food units or 40 small food units, it reproduces, adding one new bird with the same type of food-gathering mechanism. For example, if a student using tweezers gathers 10 large food units, then another student will come in off the sidelines and participate in the next

TEACHER SECTION

feeding cycle. The new student also uses tweezers, just as his or her "parent" bird.

For the next season, the Evolutionary Biologist will add new food, doubling the amount of remaining food (by adding one grain or one pea for each that remains). In this second round, each surviving bird (original plus any new offspring) gets 20 seconds of feeding. Each bird will take its 20-second turn individually, so all the birds are not eating at once. "Parents" should take their turn before their "offspring," and if multiple offspring are in the game, they eat in order of oldest to youngest (first to join the game, second to join the game, etc.).

Continue this rotation until each player in the habitat has fed. The Evolutionary Biologist should record on the *Data Sheet* all food units gathered for the second generation. Continue for at least one more generation, although the more generations the class plays, the more the idea of competition and limited resources will be emphasized.

Results

After the game is complete, have the students graph their results. Let them be creative—they can graph generations, number of birds, amount of food eaten, finger-finches vs. tweezer-finches, average per generation, average per person, etc. These varying graphs should launch a discussion of what the results indicate about natural selection of the birds as well as the natural selection of the plants themselves, changes in environmental conditions, and the influence of competition in natural selection.

Standards

The material promoted in this activity enhances and supports student understanding of the following *National Science Education Standards* for grades 5–8:

Diversity and Adaptations of Organisms (Life Science)

Millions of species of animals, plants, and microorganisms are alive today. Although different species might look dissimilar, the unity among organisms becomes apparent from an analysis of internal structures, the similarity of their chemical processes, and the evidence of common ancestry.

Biological evolution accounts for the diversity of species developed through gradual processes over many generations. Species acquire many of their unique characteristics through biological adaptation, which involves the selection of naturally occurring variations in populations. Biological adaptations include changes in structures, behaviors, or physiology that enhance survival and reproductive success in a particular environment.

Extinction of a species occurs when the environment changes and the adaptive characteristics of a species are insufficient to allow its survival. Fossils indicate that many organisms that lived long ago are extinct. Extinction of species is common; most of the species that have lived on the Earth no longer exist.

Assessment

Activity	Exemplary	Emergent	Deficient
	After the game is complete, the students graph their results accurately and are able to discuss what the results indicate about natural selection of the birds, their food sources, changes in environmental conditions, and the influence of competition.	After the game is complete, the students need help graphing their results. They have some trouble discussing what the results indicate about natural selection of the birds, their food sources, changes in environmental conditions, and the influence of competition.	Students cannot graph their results or discuss the meaning of the simulation.

BATTLE OF THE BIRD BEAKS

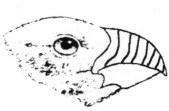

The purpose of this activity is to show the effect of competition for resources and natural selection. Your teacher will assign you into a few teams of three, and the rest of the students will watch from the sidelines, until they have a chance to be "born" into the game.

1. For each starting team, your teacher will assign one member to be the project Evolutionary Biologist who will manage the game and record the results. The other two team members will be birds—finches—like those on the Galápagos Islands and those you studied in an earlier activity. For this activity, there will be two types of finches, those with large beaks and those with small beaks.

   If you are a large-beaked finch, you will use your fingers as your beak to pick up food. You can only pick up food by pinching two fingers together to get a grain of rice or a pea. If you are a small-beaked finch, you will use tweezers as your beak.

   Regardless of which type of finch you are, you may pick up only one piece of food at a time. Once you pick up a piece of food, you must deposit it in a paper cup before getting another piece of food. You will only be able to eat during a "feeding season" that lasts 20 seconds. During that time, you need to collect enough food to survive.

2. Collect the materials from your teacher, including a patterned cloth, rice, peas, and tweezers. The patterned cloth represents a habitat the finches occupy in the Galápagos. Other groups in the class may have a differently patterned cloth to represent a different habitat. The Evolutionary Biologist will randomly distribute 100 peas and 200 grains of rice on the cloth.

3. When all the teams are ready, the teacher will start a "feeding season" for 20 seconds. The finch sitting to the right of the Evolutionary Biologist will go first. During that time, you will pick up as many food units as possible, but you can select only one piece of food at a time, and you can only use either your fingers or your tweezers, depending on what type of finch you are. You must drop the food into your cup before getting another piece of food.

4. After the first finch has fed, the second finch will do the same.

BATTLE OF THE BIRD BEAKS

5. At the end of each feeding season (turn), count how many of each food type you selected. The Evolutionary Biologist will record this on the *Data Chart*. If you have gathered 10 large food units or 20 small food units (or any combination—one large food unit equals two small food units), then you survive to the next round.

   If you do not gather enough food, you need to leave the habitat and join the rest of the students on the sidelines waiting to be "born."

6. For every set of food units (10 large or 20 small units, in any combination) you gather, you will survive and be able to gather food in the next feeding season. However, if you get enough food, not only will you survive, you will reproduce! Once you get 20 large food units or 40 small food units (in any combination), another bird will be added to your team. The new bird will have the same type of food-gathering mechanism (fingers or tweezers) as you do.

7. For the next season the Evolutionary Biologist will add more food units to the cloth. He or she will double the number of remaining food units by adding one food unit for each type that remains (so if there are 9 grains of rice and 5 peas left over, you will add 9 more grains of rice and 5 more peas, making a total of 18 grains of rice and 10 peas ready at the start of the new season).

8. In the next season there will again be 20 seconds of feeding for each bird (original birds that survived, plus any new offspring). Each bird will take its turn of 20 seconds of feeding, then the next player will feed. Instead of starting with the player to the right of the Evolutionary Biologist, now the "oldest" birds will feed. Start with the same two birds that were in the last round. If they now have offspring, the offspring wait to feed until the others have fed. Offspring then eat in the order in which they were born. Continue this rotation until each player has fed.

9. At the end of the round, the Evolutionary Biologist should record all food units gathered on the data sheet for the second generation.

10. Continue rounds of feeding seasons, repeating the steps above until the teacher tells you to stop.

11. At the end of the activity, plot your data on a graph as instructed by your teacher.

DATA CHART

Student Name & Type of Finch	Generation 1		Generation 2		Generation 3	
	# of small units	# of large units	# of small units	# of large units	# of small units	# of large units
1.						
2.						
3.						
4.						
5.						
6.						
7.						
TOTAL:						

FINCH BEAKS:
IT'S IN THE GENES

Background Information

In Darwin's journals he writes about the now-famous Galápagos finches:

Of land-birds I obtained 26 kinds, all peculiar to the group [of islands] and found nowhere else, with the exception of one lark-like finch from North America (Dolichonyx oryzivorus), which ranges on that continent as far north as 54°, and generally frequents marshes.... The remaining land-birds form a most singular group of finches, related to each other in the structure of their beaks, short tails, form of body and plumage...

Darwin described natural selection as the fact that each individual organism varies, and many more organisms are born than can possibly survive. For example, in *Origin of Species*, he calculated that the offspring of a single pair of elephants could number at least 15 million after 500 years. Although Darwin did not understand the mechanisms of individual variation (genetic variability of offspring as a result of mutation and the recombination of genes) when he proposed the idea of natural selection, he emphasized the importance of this variability on the survival of the organisms.

Because of the finite nature of natural resources in any ecosystem, the variability of these organisms caused some to be better able to survive, while others perished more quickly. Those that survived, of course, are more likely to reproduce and have offspring with similar traits, possibly be better able to survive in their generation, and again be more likely to reproduce.

Darwin understood that some changes in a population do not enhance the organisms' ability to survive, and in fact could actually lower their ability to survive, but these variations would likely soon be selected out of existence. Through natural selection the enhanced individuals survive, and perhaps surpass, the others of their species. In some cases these changes may allow an individual to occupy a different niche from other organisms in a population. If organisms that have adapted to a new environmental niche

Objectives

- To understand the genetic principles that help maintain stability of populations and allow for the variations that, through natural selection, cause a population or species to adapt to environmental changes.

- To understand how a particular trait can be selected against by natural selection, yet the allele that determines the trait is still maintained within the population.

Materials

- Student handouts:

    Dominance in Beaks (Part A)
    Non-Dominance in Beaks (Part B)
    Natural Selection vs. Genetic Stability (Part C)

    Data Sheet

- 150 dried red colored beans (~1 lb per class)

- 150 dried white colored beans (~1 lb per class)

- Six plastic cups in three pairs of colors (e.g., two blue, two yellow, two green)

- Graph paper (optional)

- Pens and pencils

ACTIVITY 19: FINCH BEAKS—IT'S IN THE GENES!

TEACHER SECTION

cannot or do not reproduce with organisms in the original population, then eventually a new species will form (evolve).

This activity is a model that will help students understand the genetic principles that help maintain stability of populations and allow for variations. Through natural selection, these variations cause a population or species to adapt to environmental changes. Students are introduced to a simplified explanation for beak variability. You should make it clear that the genetics that control the size of the beak in finches is much more complicated than this simplified model. However, even though this activity is simplistic, it is representative of the concepts that govern both population stability and variation.

For the purpose of this activity, you will need to make several assumptions. First is that the heritability of finch beak size is high; that is, inheritance controls beak size more than the environmental factors (food, water, etc.).

Second, assume that the beak of the medium ground finch is controlled by a single gene, which has two variants (B) and (b), known as alleles. The (B) allele will be represented by a single red bean, and the (b) allele will be represented by a single white bean. The alleles will combine into a paired genotype, in this case (BB), (Bb), or (bb), for each finch that we study. In our simplified model, the gene pair will control the beak size of the finch.

In Part B, the model assumes a different mechanism for beak size—no dominance. In this activity finches with (BB) still have large beaks and those with (bb) have small beaks, but finches with (Bb) have intermediate beaks.

Part C focuses upon the selection factor of natural selection. The genetic mechanism from Parts A or B can be used, but any birds that are born with small beaks will starve to death when no small seeds are left on the island. Part C assumes only genetic variability as the cause of various beak sizes; one of the major causes of variation in species—random mutation—is not considered in this activity for simplicity's sake.

The purpose of the three parts is to show how various beak sizes can be maintained even in an environment that selects against a particular gene type. Students should be able to show how populations can vary but still maintain genes that are selected against by the environment.

Procedure

Divide the class into groups of two to four students. Be sure to convey that the beans represent alleles of a single gene, and that (in this case) each parent provides one allele to the offspring. If your students are not already familiar with Punnet squares, this may be a good time to introduce the concept. You can use Punnet squares to predict the results of Parts A, B, and C, and then have your students compare their results to the predicted ratios.

Part A: Dominance in Beaks

In this section, the model assumes that the gene for large beaks (B) is dominant over the gene for small beaks (b) in the medium ground finch. For example, a finch that is homozygous (BB) has a large beak, a finch that is homozygous (bb) will have a small beak, and the heterozygous genotype (Bb) also has the dominant trait—large beaks.

1. Have students in each group put 20 red beans in one blue cup and 20 white beans in a second blue cup. Each cup represents one parent in Generation 1—the cup with red beans is a large-beaked finch; the cup with white beans is a small-beaked finch. The fact that both cups are blue shows they are in the same generation. See illustration for guidance.

2. To "reproduce" Generation 2, groups will select one allele (bean) from each cup as the gene pair of each parental bird. In Table 1 on the *Data Sheet*, students will record the genotype (red/red = BB, red/white = Bb, or white/white = bb) and phenotype (large- or small-beaked) for each new finch (pair of genes). They will soon catch on that all offspring will be heterozygous (Bb) and therefore large-beaked. After recording this data, they should put half the bean pairs in each yellow cup, resulting in 20 beans (10 red and 10 white) per cup.

3. For Generation 3, each student in the group will take turns selecting a pair of beans, one from each yellow cup. They should select the bean without looking into the cup so the color selection is random. The students should note the data in Table 1 of the *Data Sheet*, recording the genotype of each pair as it is selected: BB (red/red), Bb (red/white), and bb (white/white). Team members continue picking bean pairs until all the beans have been selected. They should put the selected beans to the side until they are ready to begin the next section.

TEACHER SECTION

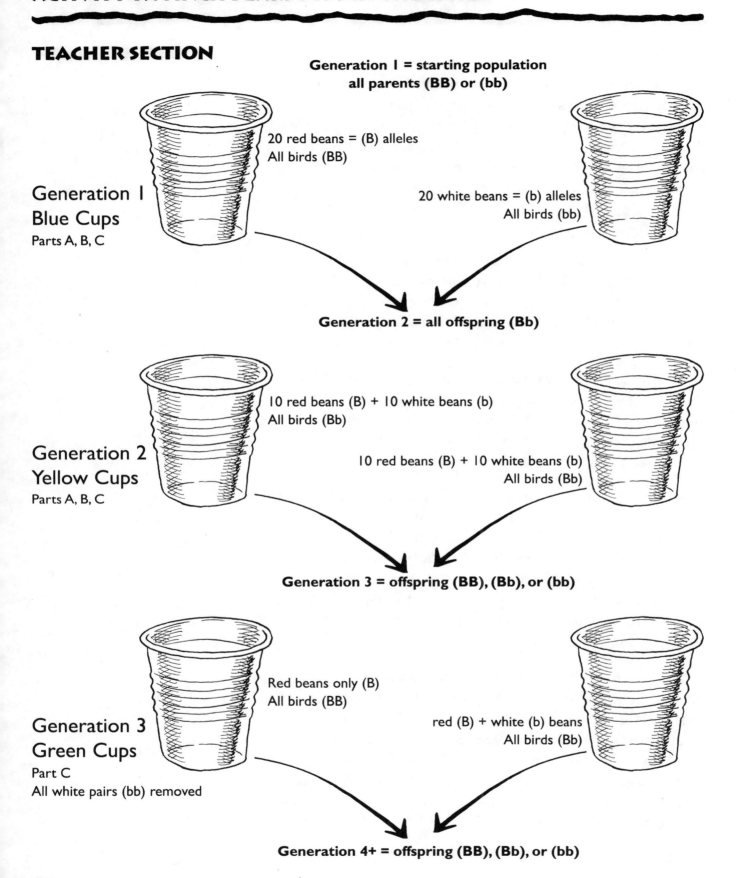

**Generation 1 = starting population
all parents (BB) or (bb)**

20 red beans = (B) alleles
All birds (BB)

20 white beans = (b) alleles
All birds (bb)

**Generation 1
Blue Cups**
Parts A, B, C

Generation 2 = all offspring (Bb)

10 red beans (B) + 10 white beans (b)
All birds (Bb)

10 red beans (B) + 10 white beans (b)
All birds (Bb)

**Generation 2
Yellow Cups**
Parts A, B, C

Generation 3 = offspring (BB), (Bb), or (bb)

Red beans only (B)
All birds (BB)

red (B) + white (b) beans
All birds (Bb)

**Generation 3
Green Cups**
Part C
All white pairs (bb) removed

Generation 4+ = offspring (BB), (Bb), or (bb)

4. Students should then calculate Generation 3's ratio of (BB):(Bb):(bb) pairs, as well as the ratios of the beak types that are the result of the genotypes (large beaks:small beaks).

5. Following the activity, have each team report its data to the class. Make a class chart that shows the numbers of each genotype. As an option, you can have each team graph their results or create Punnet squares.

If you have discussed Punnet squares, an important point to convey to students is that the ratios predicted by the genetics are statistical. For small samples there may be a difference between actual data and anticipated data. Some of the teams may not have the expected 3:1 ratio of large-beaked to small-beaked birds.

As the number of teams reporting increases, the closer the real data comes to the predicted ratio. Ask the students why they think this is so. You may want to discuss the reasons that scientists such as Peter and Rosemary Grant have been conducting finch research on Daphne Major in the Galápagos for more than 30 years—the more observations made, the more accurate the data.

Part B: Non-Dominance in Beaks

In Part B, the model assumes that *neither* the allele for large beaks (B) nor the allele for small beaks (b) is dominant over the other. Thus, a finch that is homozygous (BB) has a large beak, a finch that is homozygous (bb) will have a small beak, and the heterozygous genotype (Bb) will have a *medium* beak.

This non-dominance type of genetics is very common in nature even though Gregor Mendel did not discuss this possibility in his pea experiments. This section should give the students the idea that genetic traits are determined by many different mechanisms in nature, and that scientists continually try to determine "rules" of inherited characteristics.

Repeat the same steps as in Part A. An important point for students to understand is that because of the random nature of the selection process, the number of homozygous and heterozygous bean pairs will be different than in Part A. In step 3, they record their results in Table 2 of the *Data Sheet*. In step 4, students calculate the ratio of genotypes resulting from phenotypes (large beaks:medium beaks:small beaks).

ACTIVITY 19: FINCH BEAKS—IT'S IN THE GENES!

TEACHER SECTION

The stability of gene frequencies within a population was proposed by mathematician G. Hardy and physician W. Weinberg; their mathematical model is known as the **Hardy-Weinberg Law**.

They demonstrated that when mating is random and no factor favors one form of the gene over another, the frequency of the genes will remain in equilibrium. Even if a particular gene type is selected against (the gene for small beaks in this activity), the gene will be maintained in the population.

The Hardy-Weinberg equilibrium states that gene frequencies will be maintained in a population only if·it is a large population with random mating, no mutations, no migration or isolation of the population, and no selection for or against a particular gene form (allele).

This simulated population of Darwin finches has an environmental selection for the gene for large beaks and against small beaks. In the natural population of medium ground finches there is also a possibility of mutations and migration of birds.

The actual Hardy-Weinberg equation ($p^2 + 2pq + q^2$) is not used in this activity, but can be investigated by advanced classes. The point of this lab is to show the effects of selection pressure on genetics.

Again, stress the difference between actual data and anticipated data. Some of the teams may not have the expected 1:2:1 ratio of large-beaked to medium-beaked to small-beaked birds. Discuss with them why the ratio for Part B is different from Part A.

Part C: Natural Selection vs. Genetic Stability

Part C will explore how genes are maintained in a mating population despite selection by the environment, in this case an La Niña drought (this explanation ties this exercise to several of the ecology activities earlier in the book).

Divide the class in half. One-half will use Part A's rules of dominance to determine the outcome, and the other half of the class will use Part B's rules of non-dominance to determine the new generations.

The objective of this activity is to show how a particular trait can be selected against by nature (natural selection), yet the allele that determines the trait is still maintained within the population. This activity demonstrates how the stability of the gene pool in a population can be influenced by environmental factors, but it does not cover gene changes due to mutation (see activity *Isolation and Adaptation: Is Survival in the Cards?*).

Both teams follow the steps for Part A (the same as for Part B) until they get to step 3. This process assumes that the parent generation—as represented by the beans in the blue cups—is not affected by the drought, but that the environment changes and affects the next generation. Explain that a drought has wiped out all of the plants that produce small seeds, so only medium and large seeds remain. Birds with small beaks will therefore starve to death because the drought has eliminated their food source. The students following Part A will have only two phenotypes (large- and small-beaked); those following Part B will have all three phenotypes.

3. To create Generation 3, each student in the group will take turns selecting a pair of beans, one from each yellow cup. They should select the bean without looking into the cup so the color selection is random. The students should note the data in Table 3 of the *Data Sheet*, recording the genotype of each pair as it is selected: BB (red/red), Bb (red/white), and bb (white/white). Each (BB) pair should be put into one green cup, each (Bb) pair into a second green cup, and each (bb) pair should be put to the side. Team members continue picking bean pairs until all the beans have been selected.

4. Students should calculate the ratio of (BB):(Bb):(bb) pairs in this generation as well as the ratios of the beak types that are the result of the genotypes. If they follow the rules of Part A, they calculate large beaks:small beaks. If they follow the rules of Part B, they calculate all three phenotypes.

5. Because all birds with a (bb) genotype died during the drought, none survived to reproduce the next generation. The beans in the green cups represent those individuals who survived the drought. For Generation 4 each student in the group will blindly select two beans, one from each green cup, and place the pair in one of three groups, recording on Table 3 of the *Data Sheet* the genotype of each pair selected: BB (red/red), Bb (red/white), and bb (white/white). Each (BB) pair should be put into one blue cup, each (Bb) pair into the second blue cup, and each (bb) pair should be put to the side (students will need to alternate the color of the cups for each generation). Team members continue picking bean pairs until all the beans have been selected.

6. Repeat step 5 for at least three more generations, removing all the small-beaked birds at the end of each turn. Make sure to record the new ratios of offspring after each generation.

Answers to student questions:

1. What happened to the allele frequencies (numbers) as a result of environmental selection? Did they stay the same? If they changed, how did they change?

    The number of (b) alleles should have been reduced in each generation, but the (b) allele is still maintained in the population.

2. What would happen to the allele frequencies if the drought ends?

    The (b) frequency should slowly increase, and finches that are born bb will survive to add their genes to the reproducing gene pool.

3. What could cause the frequency of the (b) allele to increase in the gene pool?

    Shifts in the environmental stresses, like the end of a drought such as with a La Niña, or the onset of an El Niño event that might bring increased rainfall, etc.

ACTIVITY 19: FINCH BEAKS—IT'S IN THE GENES!

TEACHER SECTION

4. What survival advantage does maintaining the (b) allele in the population give the finches?

It allows for survival if the environmental stresses suddenly shift. For example, if the increased rainfall of an El Niño caused all the plants that make large seeds to die out, or some other catastrophe occurred that affected only large- and medium-beaked finches, maintaining the (b) allele in the population allows for the possibility of small-beaked finches to survive and keep the species from going extinct.

Standards

The material promoted in this activity enhances and supports student understanding of the following *National Science Education Standards* for grades 5–8:

Reproduction and Heredity (Life Science)

Every organism requires a set of instructions for specifying its traits. Heredity is the passage of these instructions from one generation to another.

Hereditary information is contained in genes, located in the chromosomes of each cell. Each gene carries a single unit of information. An inherited trait of an individual can be determined by one or by many genes, and a single gene can influence more than one trait. A human cell contains many thousands of different genes.

The characteristics of an organism can be described in terms of a combination of traits. Some traits are inherited and others result from interactions with the environment.

Populations and Ecosystems (Life Science)

A population consists of all individuals of a species that occur together at a given place and time. All populations living together and the physical factors with which they interact compose an ecosystem.

The number of organisms an ecosystem can support depends on the resources available and abiotic factors, such as quantity of light and water, range of temperatures, and soil composition. Given adequate biotic and abiotic resources and no disease or predators, populations (including humans) increase at rapid rates. Lack of resources and other factors, such as predation and climate, limit the growth of populations in specific niches in the ecosystem.

Diversity and Adaptations of Organisms (Life Science)   **TEACHER SECTION**

Biological evolution accounts for the diversity of species developed through gradual processes over many generations. Species acquire many of their unique characteristics through biological adaptation, which involves the selection of naturally occurring variations in populations. Biological adaptations include changes in structures, behaviors, or physiology that enhance survival and reproductive success in a particular environment.

Extinction of a species occurs when the environment changes and the adaptive characteristics of a species are insufficient to allow its survival. Fossils indicate that many organisms that lived long ago are extinct. Extinction of species is common; most of the species that have lived on the Earth no longer exist.

Assessment

Activity	Exemplary	Emergent	Deficient
	Students are able to work in groups to complete each part with little teacher coaching. They follow all directions and their results are close to what is expected. They are able to discuss the basic principles of simple dominance, lack of dominance, and genetic frequency.	Students are able to work in groups to complete each part with some teacher coaching. They follow all directions and their results are close to what is expected. They have some trouble discussing the basic principles of simple dominance, lack of dominance, and genetic frequency.	Students are not able to work in groups or have trouble working in groups. Their results are not very close to what is expected. They are not able to discuss the basic principles of simple dominance, lack of dominance, and genetic frequency.

PART A

DOMINANCE IN BEAKS

In groups, you are going to study a population of Darwin finches that live on Daphne Major, a small island off the coast of Santa Cruz Island in the Galápagos Archipelago. You are going to observe how the number of finches with different types of beaks changes from one generation to the next.

In this section, your model assumes that the allele for large beaks (B) is dominant over the allele for small beaks (b) in the finch. For example, a finch that is homozygous (has two of the same allele type—BB) has a large beak, a finch that is homozygous (bb) will have a small beak, and the heterozygous genotype (has two different allele types—Bb) also has the dominant trait—large beaks.

Procedure

1. Take two blue cups to represent Generation 1 and put 20 red beans in one blue cup and 20 white beans in the other blue cup. The cup with the red beans represents birds that are homozygous and have large beaks (BB); the cup with the white beans represents birds that are homozygous and have small beaks (bb).

2. Each member of the group should take turns pulling one bean out of each blue cup. Close your eyes as you select a bean so you can't see which color you are picking. For each pair of beans pulled out, your team now has a new bird with a new genotype. Record on Table 1 of the *Data Sheet* the genotype (BB, Bb, or bb) and the phenotype (BB = large-beaked, Bb = large-beaked, and bb = small-beaked) of each new bird. After you have recorded the genotype and phenotype of each pair, put the beans in the yellow cups, placing 10 pairs in each cup. This results in 20 beans (10 red and 10 white) in each yellow cup. This is Generation 2.

3. To "reproduce" Generation 3, each member of the group should take turns blindly selecting one bean from each yellow cup. Record on Table 1 of the *Data Sheet* the genotype (BB, Bb, or bb) and the phenotype (BB = large-beaked, Bb = large-beaked, and bb = small-beaked) of each new bird. Continue picking pairs of beans until all are selected. Put the selected beans to one side; they will be used again in the next part of the activity.

4. After Generation 3 has been created from the yellow cups and Table 1 is completely filled in, calculate the ratio of genotypes (BB:Bb:bb pairs) and phenotypes that are the result of the genotypes (large beaks:small beaks) in this generation.

5. Be sure to keep orderly notes, as you will be asked to report your results to the class.

PART B
NON-DOMINANCE IN BEAKS

In this part of the activity your group will repeat exactly what you did in Part A, except now your model assumes that *neither* the allele for large beaks nor the allele for small beaks is dominant. For example, a finch that is homozygous (BB) has a large beak, a finch that is homozygous (bb) will have a small beak, but a finch that has the heterozygous genotype (Bb) will have an intermediate, or *medium* beak.

Procedure

1. Take two blue cups to represent Generation 1 and put 20 red beans in one blue cup and 20 white beans in the other blue cup. The cup with the red beans represents birds that are homozygous and have large beaks (BB); the cup with the white beans represents birds that are homozygous and have small beaks (bb).

2. Each member of the group should take turns pulling one bean out of each blue cup. Close your eyes as you select a bean so you can't see which color you are picking. For each pair of beans pulled out, your team now has a new bird with a new genotype. Record on Table 2 of the *Data Sheet* the genotype (BB, Bb, or bb) and the phenotype (BB = large-beaked, Bb = medium-beaked, and bb = small-beaked) of each new bird. After you have recorded the genotype and phenotype of each pair, put the beans in the yellow cups, placing 10 pairs in each cup. This results in 20 beans (10 red and 10 white) in each yellow cup. This is Generation 2.

3. To "reproduce" Generation 3, each member of the group should take turns blindly selecting one bean from each yellow cup. Record on Table 2 of the *Data Sheet* the genotype (BB, Bb, or bb) and the phenotype (BB = large-beaked, Bb = medium-beaked, and bb = small-beaked) of each new bird. Continue picking pairs of beans until all are selected. Put the selected beans to one side; they will be used again in the next part of the activity.

4. After a new generation of birds has been created from the yellow cups and Table 2 is completely filled in, calculate the ratio of genotypes (BB:Bb:bb pairs) and phenotypes that are the result of the genotypes (large beaks:medium beaks:small beaks) in this generation.

5. Be sure to keep orderly notes, as you will be asked to report your results to the class.

PART C
NATURAL SELECTION VS. GENETIC STABILITY

In this part of the activity, your group will explore how alleles are maintained in a mating population despite selection by the environment. Your teacher will tell you whether your group should assume that finch beaks are controlled by a dominant allele (as in Part A), or to assume that no alleles are dominant and a (Bb) combination will have a medium-sized beak (as in Part B).

The objective of this activity is to show how a particular trait can be selected against by nature (natural selection), yet the allele that determines the trait is still maintained within the population.

Procedure

Your teacher will assign your group to follow steps 1 and 2 of either Part A or Part B. Be sure to record your results from this section in Table 3 of the *Data Sheet*. After you complete step 2 from either Part A or Part B, continue with step 3 below.

3. To "reproduce" Generation 3, each member of the group should take turns blindly selecting one bean from each yellow cup. Record on Table 3 of the *Data Sheet* the genotype (BB, Bb, or bb) and the phenotype (this will depend on whether you are following the directions from Part A or Part B) of each bird. Continue picking pairs of beans until all are selected. Put each pair you select into a group, with the (BB) pairs in one group, the (Bb) pairs in another, and the (bb) pairs in a third.

4. A La Niña event occurs, causing a drought on your island, and all the plants that produce small seeds have been wiped out. Therefore, birds with small beaks that are not able to eat larger seeds die of starvation. They do not reproduce and pass on their genes to the next generation. Remove all the birds that have small beaks—(bb) beans—from your population.

5. Place each remaining group—(BB) and (Bb)—in one of the two green cups, with the homozygous birds in one cup and the heterozygous birds in another. This represents Generation 4—those birds that survived the drought.

6. For Generation 4, each member of the group should take turns selecting one bean from each green cup without looking at the beans as they are selected. Record the genotype (BB, Bb, or bb) and the phenotype (this will depend on whether you are

NATURAL SELECTION VS. GENETIC STABILITY

following the directions from Part A or Part B) in Table 3.

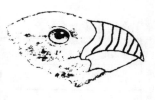

7. Repeat steps 4 through 6, again removing all the (bb) pairs from the population. This time place each of the remaining pairs into one of the blue cups, according to your teacher's directions. The blue cups represent Generation 5, again only those birds that survived the drought.

8. Repeat this process (alternating the color of cups used to keep track of the generations) for at least three more generations, removing all the small-beaked birds at the end of each turn.

9. When Table 3 is completely filled in, calculate the ratio of genotypes (BB:Bb:bb pairs) and phenotypes that are the result of the genotypes (large beaks:medium beaks:small beaks) in each generation.

10. Be sure to keep orderly notes, as you will be asked to report your results to the class.

11. Go over the following questions with your team members, and be prepared to discuss these points with your class:

1. What happened to the allele frequencies (numbers) as a result of environmental selection? Did they stay the same? If they changed, how did they change?

2. What would happen to the allele frequencies if the drought ends?

3. What could cause the frequency of the (b) allele to increase in the gene pool?

4. What survival advantage does maintaining the (b) allele in the population give the Darwin finches?

DATA SHEET

Table 1. Part A

Generation	Genotypes			Phenotypes	
	# BB	#Bb	#bb	Big Beaks	Small Beaks
1 (Parents)	10		10	10	10
2					
3					

Table 2. Part B

Generation	Genotypes			Phenotypes		
	# BB	#Bb	#bb	Big Beaks	Med. Beaks	Small Beaks
1 (Parents)	10		10	10		10
2						
3						

Table 3. Part C

Your group follows the rules of Part _____

Generation	#BB	#Bb	#bb	Big Beaks	Medium Beaks	Small Beaks	#B alleles	#b alleles
1 (Parents)	10		10	10		10		
2								
3								
4								
5								
6								
7								
8								